Culinary Capital

Culinary Capital

Peter Naccarato and Kathleen LeBesco

London · New York

English edition
First published in 2012 by
Berg
Editorial offices:
50 Bedford Square, London WC1B 3DP, UK
175 Fifth Avenue, New York, NY 10010, USA

Reprinted 2012

Berg is an imprint of Bloomsbury Publishing Plc.

Library of Congress Cataloging-in-Publication Data

Naccarato, Peter, 1970–
Culinary capital / Peter Naccarato and Kathleen LeBesco. — English ed.
p. cm.
Includes bibliographical references and index.
ISBN 978-0-85785-415-5 (alk. paper) — ISBN 978-0-85785-382-0 (alk. paper) —
ISBN 978-0-85785-383-7 (alk. paper)   1. Food — Cross-cultural studies.
2. Food habits — Cross-cultural studies.   3. Food consumption — Cross-cultural
studies.   I. LeBesco, Kathleen, 1970–   II. Title.
GT2850.N34 2012
394.1'2–dc23
2012017458

British Library Cataloguing-in-Publication Data

A catalogue record for this book is available from the British Library.

ISBN 978 0 85785 382 0 (Cloth)
978 0 85785 383 7 (Paper)
e-ISBN 978 0 85785 415 5 (individual)

Typeset by Apex CoVantage, LLC, Madison, WI, USA.
Printed and bound in Great Britain

www.bergpublishers.com

While we eat to satisfy hunger and nourish our bodies, some of the most radical effects occur precisely when food is dissociated from eating and eating from nourishment.

—Barbara Kirshenblatt-Gimblett, "Playing to the Senses: Food as a Performance Medium"

Contents

Acknowledgements

We would like to thank a number of colleagues, students, and friends for their help in shaping this work. At Marymount Manhattan College, we appreciate the support of Dean David Podell and the late Margaret Sokol for funding for the research phase of this book. At New York University, the resources provided by the Faculty Resource Network (led by Debra Szybinski and Anne Ward) were also invaluable for research. Students in our Spring 2009 and Spring 2011 sections of "Edible Ideologies: The Politics of Food" engaged us in discussions and pushed our thinking further about the interaction of food-ways and social status. Attendees at the conferences of the National Communication Association, the Association for the Study of Food and Society, and at Crossing Borders III provided excellent feedback as we presented earlier versions of several chapters. We also appreciate thoughtful and engaged commentary provided by Kathleen Collins, Fabio Parasecoli, and several anonymous reviewers. We are grateful to the team at Berg, particularly our editor Louise Butler, for their wisdom and an efficient, nearly painless production process.

Additionally, Katie would like to thank John Shields, whose tireless and loving parenting bought her much time to write, and Molly Shields, born somewhere between the first and last drafts of this manuscript, for the simple commands ("Computer stop!" "Work done!") that pulled her back into the world.

Peter would like to thank his colleagues at Marymount for granting him the senior fellowship leave that allowed him to focus on writing, the many friends with whom he has discussed food and shared memorable meals, Anthony Naccarato, for providing us with VIP access to Wing Bowl 2010 and to the *WIP Morning Show*, and his parents, Pete and Laura Naccarato, for their continued support.

Defining Culinary Capital

Consider the following hypothetical tableau.

In Brighton, United Kingdom, Jane Smith ends her nine-hour work day. On her way home to her family, she stops by her local meal prep franchise and "whips up" chicken cacciatore. She jumps in her car, finishes the drive home, barrels into the kitchen, and opens the fridge, which is stocked with fresh fruits and vegetables that she received the night before from her online grocer. She throws together a salad, plates it with the chicken, and calls her family in to a delicious homemade meal as she beams with pride.

Meanwhile, in Tampa, Florida, José and Jennifer Santos fight for control of the remote as they flop on the couch. The compromise: he gets to watch one episode of *Iron Chef* while she gets to watch one episode of *Barefoot Contessa*. Later that evening, as they peruse the dessert menu at the upscale restaurant they've selected for dinner, Jennifer can't resist pointing out to José that she recognizes the mixed berry pavlova as one of Ina Garten's favorite desserts. José fires back with half a dozen ways to prepare mixed berries, remembering that they were the secret ingredient on *Iron Chef*. Touché—a culinary draw.

Later that evening, Jeff Liu, aka "JeffEats," hovers over his keyboard, furiously typing his review of his pilgrimage to the best dumpling shop in Vancouver's Chinatown. He launches his latest salvo in his ongoing battle with "DumplingQueenBC" over where one can find the best dumplings in the city. Satisfied with his argument that the most obscure food is the most authentic, he sits back and hits send.

The next day, Randy Rogers returns home to Topeka, having just triumphed in a three-state s'mores eating contest. With trophy in hand, he welcomes the accolades of his family, who await him with colorful hand-drawn signs cheering his victory. His neighbor, Jefferson Pettengill, asks him for an interview, which he'll post on his junk food blog. He also tells him about an upcoming eating contest—deep-fried Twinkies!—that will be held at next month's Kansas State Fair.

There is something in each of these scenes to suggest that certain food practices give people a sense of distinction within their communities, and that distinction is not based simply on how expensive things are. To make sense of food as an economic and cultural commodity, to demonstrate how a society's food practices function to circulate and challenge prevailing values and ideologies, and to understand how this is connected to the work of creating and sustaining a sense of Self, we turn to this book's organizing concept: culinary capital.

* * *

The concept of culinary capital owes a large debt to French sociologist, anthropologist, and philosopher Pierre Bourdieu, who builds upon Karl Marx's work on economic capital to understand how multiple forms of capital—economic, cultural, social, and symbolic—circulate across the social field. Bourdieu argues that by accessing these multiple forms of capital, individuals acquire status and power. To understand how this happens, Bourdieu focuses on practice, which he sees as "knit(ting) together structure and action, meaning and material conditions" (Calhoun and Sennett 2007, 7). Following Bourdieu's example, we focus particularly on how individuals' food practices are implicated in this process through the circulation of culinary capital.

Like Bourdieu, we recognize that food and food practices play a unique role as markers of social status. However, rather than presuming an inherent value stable within some culinary experiences or food products themselves and a lack of inherent value in others, we follow Bourdieu in attending to the processes through which such value is assigned and reassigned to a range of foods and food practices on a continuous and ever-changing basis. In other words, rather than assuming that culinary capital circulates in a fixed and predictable pattern (for instance, that certain foods or food practices always confer culinary capital while others do not), we focus on the multiple and potentially contradictory ways in which it may function. For example, Food Network celebrity chef Paula Deen's revelation that she has been diagnosed with diabetes has touched off debates about the recipes and foods that she promotes on her very popular programs and in her very successful cookbooks. Is it irresponsible for her to celebrate butter and other fatty foods given the potential health risks associated with them? Would the answer to this question be different if Deen were a high-end pastry chef in one of New York City's top restaurants rather than a popular media personality promoting Southern, down-home cuisine? Would the French-trained pastry chef earn culinary capital as she prepared butter-laden desserts for her restaurant's high-class clientele who relax their typical restraint in order to enjoy them, while Deen is criticized for peddling such rich foods to her presumably helpless fans? And how do different consumers use each of these types of food to position themselves in fields of status? It is the potentially conflicting answers to these types of questions that suggest the complex factors that determine how culinary capital circulates across the social landscape. At the same time, this multiplicity is exacerbated further by the need to recognize culinary capital as only one means by which individuals may construct their social identities. Thus, our goal is not to isolate culinary capital from the multidimensional social space, but rather to understand how it circulates across this cultural landscape and how it interacts with any number of prevailing values and ideologies.

It is within this context that we use the concept of culinary capital to understand how and why certain foods and food-related practices connote, and by extension, confer status and power on those who know about and enjoy them. In the mainstream United States today, for instance, a person who, in a restrained fashion, eats food produced locally and sustainably is a person with culinary capital. A person who is knowledgeable about wine and who can compare and contrast the menus at high-end restaurants has made a different, but also valuable investment in the Self, and is also rewarded with status and power. More broadly, as individuals assert the value of certain dietary preferences and food practices over others, they engage in the quest for culinary capital.

In advancing the concept of culinary capital, we extend a notion developed by Josée Johnston and Shyon Baumann (2010) in their recent foundational study of the interplay of democracy and distinction in gourmet culture. Johnston and Baumann revealed that subtle forms of social differentiation are produced by omnivorous support for both high and low food cultures. Influenced by Bourdieu, the authors chart the gourmet-ification of the culture, exploring how notions of authenticity and exoticism shape foodie discourse. Where Johnston and Baumann leave off—in examining the role of food in generating social status—we begin, offering a nuanced look at culinary capital as both a raison d'être and something that accrues in the most unpredictable of ways. In extending their work, we adapt and apply Bourdieu's ideas to consider how a variety of cultural institutions, including marketing and advertising, cable television, Internet communities, festival celebrations, and spectacular contests, function to socialize individuals. We are particularly interested in how specific cultural spaces shape individuals in dramatic ways, rewarding those who succeed with culinary capital and denying it to those who fail.

More broadly, such attempts to acquire culinary capital can be read as efforts to participate in projects of citizenship as individuals use their food practices to create and sustain identities that align with their society's norms and expectations. Our analysis of the role of culinary capital in this process is informed by the work of Michel Foucault and Nikolas Rose. Specifically, Foucault provides an important lens for understanding the role that culinary capital plays in circulating and accessing power. Using Foucault's terminology, we distinguish between oppressive and productive power, noting that while repression and prohibition play a significant role in shaping American attitudes toward food, we must also attend to the productive role of culinary capital in shaping individual identities. At the same time, we must recognize that these processes of identity formation are often implicated in the exercise of social regulation over individual behaviors and practices.

For example, through his concept of bio-power, Foucault argues that the body is a crucial site for both exercising and resisting power. In his work, Foucault emphasizes the historical and cultural transition from the body that was disciplined by the external threat of violence to the body that was shaped by individuals who sought access to power by conforming to a set of internalized values and ideologies. While Foucault does not make explicit reference to food practices and rituals in defining this concept, it is clear how they relate to it. In fact, we would argue that culinary capital plays an integral role in the "investment of power in the body" (Foucault 1980, 56), as it both promotes normative standards of the "healthy" body and also authorizes the kind of culinary indulgences and excesses that oppose such cultural expectations. Because there is no way of understanding the body in relation to power that does not take into account the very food practices and rituals through which that body is created and sustained, we recognize culinary capital as a necessary precursor to the exercise of bio-power.

Extending Foucault's work, Nikolas Rose focuses on the psychological processes through which individual identity is constructed and sustained, providing a useful context for understanding the role of culinary capital in such efforts. Specifically, he traces an important historical transformation in how citizens are governed, emphasizing a shift away from "the language of obligation, duty and social citizenship" that was the hallmark of nineteenth-century liberalism toward a discourse of free individuals who "seek to *fulfill themselves* as free individuals" (Rose 1999, 166). Such free individuals are no longer regulated by force or by a sense of obligation; rather, they act freely in a continuous effort to achieve personal fulfillment. This freedom of choice, however, does not mark the end of the governed subject; rather, it indicates a change in the technologies through which citizens are governed. Specifically, it raises the question of how individuals are to be regulated if they are going to exercise such freedom of choice. According to Rose, the answer is that rather than using the threat of punishment to force citizens to make specific choices, individuals begin to govern themselves by choosing to adopt specific practices and behaviors because of the status that comes with doing so.

Relating Rose's ideas specifically to food, while consumers are presumably free to make their own choices regarding their preferred food-related practices, such freedom of choice is always influenced by a set of cultural norms and values that have been internalized by those consumers. Thus, society does not regulate individual behavior through external restrictions on consumers' choices; rather, it relies upon a model of citizenship in which consumers curtail their own freedom of choice in order to conform to their society's expectations and thereby be identified as good citizens. Essentially, maintaining good eating practices—as defined within the context of one's culture—has become an indicator of being a good citizen. One might take, for instance, Michael Pollan's rules about "how to eat" as a set of guidelines for producing good citizens. As individuals learn to avoid foods that won't eventually rot and to always leave the table a little hungry, for example, they begin to accumulate culinary capital and in doing so self-identify as good citizens. People neither follow these rules out of a fear of overt punishment, nor do they engage with them out of a sense of duty or obligation. Rather, they usually aim, of their own volition, for personal fulfillment, making efforts to improve themselves as they take on the making of the self as a project (Rose 1999, 166).

Extending this example, the exalted status of the good home cook, the locavore shopper, the armchair restaurant critic, and the knowledgeable food television viewer alike emerges because they each engage in food-related practices that reflect a certain set of values that are privileged over others. Surely, the attitudes about food that permeate contemporary American society have their repressive and prohibitive elements; the United States is, after all, a diet-crazed society that at times seems to revel in the severe regulation of individual desires. At the same time, such food-related attitudes and assumptions can also be quite productive: they produce knowledge, induce pleasure, and generate power (Foucault 1990, 73). In contexts like these, individuals are active participants in their own empowerment through their search for self-realization. It is within this framework that we read food and food practices in relation to projects of the Self and, in doing so, witness culinary capital in action.

At the same time, active participation in one's own empowerment cannot go unchecked. In short, we are interested in how the concept of culinary capital provides a framework for understanding how an individual's food choices function simultaneously as an exercise in freedom and as a means of containing it. However, rather than assuming that food practices must always be read as signaling conformity to culinary and cultural norms and values, we are equally interested in moments when resistance is afoot.

Our approach to culinary resistance is also informed by Bourdieu, who recognizes that foodways are one arena in which the working class challenge the power of the upper and middle classes. As peasants and workers indulge together in disregard of cultural edicts surrounding sobriety and slimness, they assert a different set of values and priorities. We argue that this peasant revolt against a narrowly conceived culinary capital finds itself played out in a number of cultural sites, including those that we explore in chapter 5. In fact, we argue that while one means of acquiring culinary capital is to approach one's food practices in ways that conform to prevailing attitudes and assumptions about food and foodways—thus contributing to one's identification as a "good citizen"—an alternative is to endorse or engage in eating practices that appear to contradict or challenge such norms.

As contemporary American society becomes increasingly focused on a set of normative values surrounding culinary choices and practices, we are interested in people who use food and foodways to fight back, to question and undermine these social censorships and unhinge economic resources from pleasure and taste. Are they peripheral to mainstream American culture and as such should be excluded from cultural analysis? Or, in neglecting them, do we risk ignoring crucial sites for the production and circulation of an alternative model of culinary capital?

If Bourdieu compels us to recognize culture as produced through practice—as "embodied, engaged, interactive, creative, and contested" (Calhoun and Sennett 2007, 5)—then it is imperative to ask which kinds of practice warrant our attention. While chapters 2 through 4 explore how culinary capital functions hegemonically as it circulates across cultural sites that encourage consumers to approach their food choices and practices in ways that conform to prevailing attitudes and assumptions about food and foodways, we transition in chapter 5 to consider sites that promote eating practices that appear to contradict or challenge such norms while offering their own form of culinary capital to those who embrace them. Rather than assuming that such sites, and the practices that they promote, must be read negatively or that those who visit them and engage in such practices lack the knowledge or will-power that would direct them to "proper" or "healthier" choices, we argue that such sites, and the practices that they promote, assume a complex relationship with the mainstream discourses they seem to challenge.

Our approach is informed, in part, by Warren Belasco's analysis of the "countercuisine," which he frames within the broader context of "subcultural dissent and deviancy" (Belasco 2005, 219). First and foremost, Belasco underscores the relationship between food choices and social categories as he articulates the link between dietary choices and both individual and group identity formation: "By categorizing foods into what's good to eat and what is not, a cuisine helps a society's members define themselves: To eat appropriate foods is to participate in a particular group; eat inappropriate foods and you're an outsider. Like language, a cuisine is a medium by which a society establishes its special identity" (Belasco 1989, 44). In focusing on the "countercuisine" that emerged in the United States in the 1960s, Belasco considers the potential impact of those individuals and groups who challenge their society's prevailing culinary attitudes and trends. Rather than assuming that they have little impact given the economic, political, and ideological power of the mainstream, Belasco traces a much more nuanced process by which the countercuisine's attitudes about food and its preferred culinary practices, which had been deemed "deviant" by mainstream American culture, gradually influenced evolving American foodways, as evidenced by "organic farms, coops, farmers markets, natural foods supermarket chains, New American Cuisine restaurants, and designer bread boutiques that feed some of us today" (Belasco 2005, 223). By offering a compelling critique of the economic, political, and ideological conditions that promote this changing American food landscape, Belasco provides a crucial framework for understanding the relationship between cultures and subcultures, the mainstream and the marginal, compliance and resistance. Most importantly, he provides a framework for challenging the assumption that "resistance is futile" as he demonstrates the gradual but effectual process through which this "countercuisine" has found its way into the mainstream of contemporary American attitudes and assumptions about food and food practices.

When applied to our analysis of sites at which prevailing attitudes and assumptions about food and foodways are resisted, Belasco's work provides a framework for understanding how those who engage in "deviant" food practices can impact the mainstream culinary norms and trends that they challenge while staking their own claim to culinary capital. Rather than assuming that the larger social field is immune from those individuals or marginal groups whose choices and behaviors deviate from its prescribed course, we are interested in how both the culinary landscape and the values that shape it are not only challenged but potentially reshaped by such outliers.

DEFINING PRIVILEGED PRACTICES: HOW AMERICANS (SHOULD) EAT

Culinary capital is intricately linked to economic capital and the class-based hierarchy that it supports; however, it is important to understand that its influence extends well beyond this particular field. As Johnston and Baumann point out, "while our taste in food continues to speak to our class position, this is not a simple correspondence between rarefied 'fancy' food for high-class people, but a more complex, omnivorous affair" (2010, xx). In focusing our analysis on how culinary capital supports what could be identified as a middle-class identity, we recognize that such an identity is usually conflated with pure economic status, but there is more to this story. Great numbers of people cling and aspire to middle-class identity, even as the economic ground under their feet, inflected by unemployment, racial discrimination, and general inequality (Pattillo 2010), shifts.

Beyond its complicated connection to economic status, culinary capital also serves as a bellwether for a range of prevailing values and ideologies, including normative attitudes and assumptions about race, gender, sexuality, and ethnicity. In short, it is often implicated in sustaining within contemporary

American culture the image of an idealized middle class that is white, masculine, and heterosexual. As such, it functions to fuel the aspirations of the lower class while shunning the elitism of the upper class and thus emerges as the foundation upon which American society is built. Culinary capital is, in effect, performed as part of a middle-class ideal—a status effect of routine engagement in activities and labor understood to have class value. Christopher Carrington describes gender as a "dynamic and purposeful accomplishment; something people produce in social interaction" (Carrington 2008, 274), which is also an apt way of understanding culinary capital. Rather than an overdetermined display of a particular economic reality, it is a performance. While culinary trends may be influenced by and in some instances aspire to upper-class elitism, they are also shaped by strong American impulses toward self-improvement and democratization. Therefore, rather than understanding culinary capital as the birthright of the upper class and thus firmly ensconced at the top of this class-based hierarchy, we argue that it circulates much more freely. As it does so, it provides a means of negotiating the often conflicted priorities of the upper and lower classes while stabilizing the middle class by promoting what are identified as its, and thus American, principles and values.

Among upper-middle class Americans, whose foodways have set something of a bar for middle-class consumption practices, recent years have witnessed an uptick in food-related discourse and preoccupation with a different form of "conspicuous consumption" than that which sociologist Thorstein Veblen had in mind in *Theory of the Leisure Class* (1899). No longer is one limited to demonstrating one's sophistication and worldliness by importing pricey, domestically unavailable products or by dining out at upscale bastions of traditionalism like The 21 Club or The Russian Tea Room. Today, the upper-middle class in America also makes its name by consuming conspicuously, yet carefully, with an eye toward criteria unheard of a few decades ago. Food quality is now determined less by abundant quantity and global provenance and more by sourcing (the more local, the better), artisanality (the smaller the run, the better), taste (with organic methods favored), sustainability, healthiness, and the mindfulness with which it is eaten. Former editor of *Gourmet* Ruth Reichl intones, "My idea of good living is not about eating high on the hog. Rather, to me good living means understanding how food connects us to the earth" (Solomon 2009, 18). Consumers who want to establish their own identities as contemporary foodies can do so by making or appearing to make their own food choices using criteria similar to those espoused by Reichl. As we discuss in the chapters that follow, this is precisely part of the logic by which popular trends like meal assembly kitchens and online grocers (chapter 2), televised food programming (chapter 3), and online restaurant review sites (chapter 4) market themselves to consumers eager to stake their claim to the culinary capital enjoyed by Reichl and those like her who have achieved cult-like status across today's privileged foodscape.

Best-selling food writers like Reichl, Michael Pollan, Marion Nestle, and Barbara Kingsolver feed a hungry, aspirational readership the notion that transparency is a virtue, suggesting that food should be information-dense and that eaters must do due diligence to ensure that the stories their food tells are the right ones. When their critics grouse about elitism, arguing that the food practices that would provide a happy ending to these stories cost dearly and are inaccessible for poor and working-class people, the authors respond with charges of naïveté about the *real* costs of food. Pollan, for example, explains that "our food system depends on consumers' not knowing much about it beyond the price disclosed at the checkout scanner. Cheapness and ignorance are mutually reinforcing" (2006, 245). From pointing out that "petroleum is one of the most important ingredients in the production of modern meat" (2006, 83) to emphasizing "farming's role in global warming" (2006, 198), Pollan seeks to expose the political, economic, and environmental costs behind the "cheap" food that dominates the American diet. By doing so, Pollan and others cast individual food choice within a broader moral framework in which those who possess culinary capital can justify their position by judging, condemning, or patronizing those who do not make "the right choices" when it comes to food. In contrast, we argue in chapter 5 that those who eschew organic, reject local, and abstain from artisanal require closer analysis as they privilege an alternative set of criteria for acquiring culinary capital.

At the same time, the elite foodways prescribed by Pollan and others are not the only formulae for attaining culinary capital. Rather, a newer model based on choice and flexibility dovetails with the concept of "omnivorousness," originated by Richard Peterson (1997) and elaborated upon by Alan Warde, Lydia Martens and Wendy Olsen (1999) as well as Johnston and Baumann (2010). We utilize this concept in chapter 4 to understand a crucial shift in how individual culinary choices play a role in creating and sustaining an individual's sense of Self. In an economy marked by ever-expanding consumerism and consumption, what becomes a mark of distinction is not the exclusiveness of one's tastes or choices but rather, an individual's openness to a range of experiences. Those who seek out the greatest variety of tastes and who are open to the broadest range of experiences emerge as the most culturally capitalized. While such choices may initially seem available to all individuals within an affluent society, thus suggesting a democratizing impulse behind this shift from elitism to omnivorousness, Reay Tannahill reminds us that such a breadth of choices is itself a marker of class status: "Food flexibility (as a matter of choice) is usually a characteristic of affluent societies. The nearness of hunger breeds conservatism. Only the well-fed can afford to try something new, because only they can afford to leave it on the plate if they dislike it" (1973, 393). Thus, when applied to dietary choices, omnivorousness, like the culinary elitism it eschews, serves as a sign of culinary capital.

Rather than suggesting that the contemporary American food scene is shaped exclusively by either the discourse of elitism or omnivorousness, we are interested in how these seemingly contradictory discourses act side by side to sustain a set of privileged attitudes about food and food practices. Specifically, despite their apparent differences, it is clear that both models are available only to those with the economic resources and cultural capital to adopt them. It is evident that both perspectives rely on a form of class-based elitism, which Joseph Epstein argues, "sets in when much more seems at stake than the taste of the food on the table" (2002, 219). He traces the roots of contemporary trends in culinary snobbery to 1970s-era foreign travel, interest in ethnic food, growth of supermarkets, spread of vegetarianism, national obsession with healthy eating, and never-ending concern about diet and nutrition (Epstein 2002, 217). He also links it to socioeconomic status: "A social-class phenomenon this healthful eating turns out to be, for the adults who do eat what they like and in the quantities they want are almost always of . . . the lower orders. We see them in McDonald's or Taco Bell . . . scarfing up one or another sort of flavorful yet one expects deadly dish. . . . Happy wretches, they remind one of no people so much as the Epsilons in Aldous Huxley's *Brave New World*: gross, misshapen, deliberately underbred to do society's drone work, and deprived of all insight into the reasons for their own being. They shall die early, we think, the cause of death being lower-class ignorance, poor creatures. Distinctly not People Like Us" (Epstein 2002, 223–224). This chillingly familiar scene dramatizes the link between food choices and identity formation—"they" eat fast food; "they" make bad choices; "they" will die young and ignorant; "they" are not "us."

While Epstein assumes a critical stance against those who would espouse such culinary elitism, other authors marshal such class-based prejudices in the service of stinging critiques of populism (culinary and otherwise). Robert Corfe writes of a "poison of populism" that "is in direct opposition to the progress of society" and thus "needs to be addressed" (2007, v). According to Corfe, such populism undergirds all of our ills: "Out of the hybrid and stinking stew which constitutes America has not only emerged a nation which is at war with the civilized values demanded by humanity at its best, but a nation intent on pulling down the peoples of the world to its own level of incivility and coarseness" (2007, vii). Corfe vociferously condemns any movement by the people that works in opposition to elite cultural values and practices (an attitude that is echoed in the condemnations of competitive eating that we discuss in chapter 5). At first glance, it seems as though the movement toward omnivorousness, with its rejection of the very elitism that Corfe embraces, would fit in here as it contributes to the cultural decay that he fears. However, even as it promotes a cultural and culinary flexibility that Corfe would condemn, it simultaneously promotes its own form of culinary elitism.

In fact, both the overt elitism of a foodscape marked by exclusion and privilege and the covert elitism of a foodscape shaped by omnivorousness find expression in some of today's most influential writers on food policy and practices. On the one hand, those in the know argue that the masses can be saved by limiting their food practices and choices to those prescribed by the culinary elite, in short, by eschewing populism in favor of culinary elitism. Michael Pollan, like Eric Schlosser, argues that, after all, "A great many social movements begin with the elite. Just because a movement is elitist, we shouldn't dismiss it. The abolition and women's suffrage movements were 'elitist.' The elite have more time and freedom to deal with some of these issues. If a movement stays elitist, though, that's a problem" (quoted in Wagenvoord 2004). Thus, commands from on high, like Pollan's rules to "Eat food. Not too much. Mostly plants" (2009, 1), are designed to guide the plebs toward eating practices that will ensure not only their own health and well-being, but that of the planet as well.

On the other hand, the contemporary food scene extols a culinary adventurism that crosses such boundaries, embraces a full range of culinary experiences, and celebrates omnivorousness. Such adventurism serves to Other non-white cultures by making their food, and thus them, exotic and something to be consumed or mastered by the foodie (hooks 1992). Jeffrey Steingarten, food critic for *Vogue*, writes skeptically about the "irrational food phobias" (including "genetic inheritance, allergy, vegetarianism, matters of taste, nutrition, food safety, obesity, or a sensitive nature") that keep people from sharing all sorts of food with one another, and urges human omnivores to reconnect to the delicious bounties of nature (1996).

By bridging seemingly contradictory discourses of selectivity and omnivorousness, popular food writers, taken as a whole, have subtly balanced elitism and a particular form of populism in formulating their ideal culinary landscape. But while popular culture imposed from "above" is constituted as such, what everyday people do with these ideas on the ground is far from overdetermined. There is often a productive antagonism between those "in the know" who promote privileged culinary practices that prioritize sustainability, health, and dietary restraint, or who prescribe specific gender roles for men and women, and those who seem to reject these criteria in their foodways. While the educational advice rendered by these would-be food prophets is aimed at improving individual and global health, there are problematic undertones to much of their work. More specifically, as Anna Kirkland has noted in her attempts to challenge anti-obesity policy, such policy too often reflects incorrect assumptions about health, and dabbles in moralism, resulting in interventions that are punitive, ineffective, and patronizing. What is typically overlooked is the need for structural change and broad redistribution of resources (Kirkland 2011, 411), particularly with an eye toward the racial implications of current distribution systems and models. On the other hand, as we discuss in chapter 5, the resistance to privileged food practices espoused by some proponents of junk food and competitive eating is also problematic, aligning with the corporate mantras of Big Food, willfully inviting disease and illness, and trafficking in the unsustainable.

This book seeks to tackle a culinary elitism that assumes the intellectual and moral superiority of those who resist the ubiquitous temptations of the industrial food system and that stigmatizes those it views as lacking discipline and self-control. In a departure from Johnston and Baumann, who reveal the tango between the pursuit of social status and the awareness of social inequality implicit in foodie discourse, we locate and analyze "sites of resistance." In the United States, these are places like state fairs and carnivals, competitive eating contests, and "junk" food blogs where individuals seemingly reject the privileged values of sustainability, heath, and restraint that permeate today's food scene in favor of unhealthy and excessive eating. In short, we plumb anti-foodie discourse for its own internal tensions and deeper meanings, and find a topsy-turvy investment in culinary capital. However, we do so respectful of the agency of citizens who make individual dietary choices and mindful of the subtle ways in which those choices are necessarily influenced by a range of ideologies and on-the-ground conditions.

CONTEXTUALIZING CULINARY CAPITAL

While we argue that culinary capital is especially and increasingly valued in contemporary American culture, we are not suggesting that it originated there. Rather, we stipulate that all cultures use food and food practices as a way of conferring cultural authority and circulating dominant ideologies just as their citizens may use them to both reinforce and transgress their culture's norms and values. In fact, one can identify the cultural significance and ideological function of food and food-related practices across histories and cultures.

While the chapters that follow explore culinary capital in a number of key sites in contemporary American culture, we recognize the historical and cultural specificity of our investigation but also highlight the extent to which similar studies could focus on any number of histories and cultures. The sites we explore are not isolated entities: meal assembly businesses exist not only in the United States, but also in Canada and the United Kingdom (though their numbers are in decline), and e-grocers are a growing business in North America, Asia, and the United Kingdom. U.S.-based cookery programs, online restaurant review communities, and blogs celebrating "junk" food have their parallels in dozens of other countries with similar media infrastructure. And although "state" fairs are specifically American, carnivals and fetes in which food figures prominently are a global phenomenon. While culinary capital circulates in specific and complex ways throughout contemporary American culture, its reach certainly extends well beyond the historical and cultural moment that grounds our study. As such, we cannot overlook the transhistorical and cross-cultural nature of culinary capital especially given the fact that we undertake this analysis at a historical moment when a range of economic and political crises around food have garnered significant attention. While this study does not engage extensively with these important debates, they necessarily impact American attitudes toward food and, thus, frame our analysis.

The global financial crisis of 2008, just months on the heels of food riots in many developing nations, underscores the fact that an exploration of food as an economic and cultural commodity in the United States in the early twenty-first century must be situated within a transnational and cross-cultural context. With many world economies lacking food sovereignty and facing deep financial crises, one might assume that the symbolic value of food and food practices has diminished as we confront a different set of questions: *whether* one can produce and access food rather than *what kind* and *what level of taste it signifies.*

In other words, a shift in focus from the cultural consumption of food to its material production and distribution could be read as the death knell for culinary capital. However, rather than concluding that food and food practices can be analyzed *either* through the lens of consumption *or* production depending upon economic conditions at a particular historical moment, we argue that both perspectives are necessary for understanding how food and foodways circulate both materially and symbolically in a global context in which culinary capital affirms economic and cultural status across and between nations. Our work here hinges on the conviction that culinary capital in food-secure domains like the middle-class United States not only serves to shape individual identity, but increasingly to shape national status as well. Consequently, culinary capital plays a role in separating and stratifying countries based on the extent to which they *aspire to* particular, favored foodways, sometimes apart from the actual food practices in which they engage.

One consequence of this creation of "national" identities is that it covers up important intra-national differences. A model, for instance, that sees the United States as a relatively food secure first-world nation in comparison to second- and third-world nations that face food shortages and riots ignores the significant differences within the United States between those who enjoy absolute food security and those who struggle to feed themselves and their families, particularly in the context of the recession. Such an erasure hides class- and race-based hierarchies in the United States that warrant deeper examination. Thus, we are careful to note that our focus on the "middle-class United States" does not presume that all Americans are middle class and food secure. In fact, alarming numbers of people are not food secure.

The very U.S. foodways that confer culinary capital were not conceived in a vacuum but are, in many important ways, the result of interactions between the United States and other nations, between the mainstream and the subculture, between the "developed" and "developing." At the level of individual and group identity construction, Lisa Heldke discusses "food adventurers," noting that culinary forays into Otherness confer distinction for an educated middle class who "snobbishly see ourselves as above the hoi polloi" but who must "mark that status with cultural indicators that don't require overlarge incomes" (2003, xxiii). At the level of national and transnational identity formation, Raj Patel, Eric Holt-Gimenez, and Annie Shattuck (2009) critique efforts by the Bill and Melinda Gates Foundation to address African food shortages for assuming that African farmers suffer from a "deficit of knowledge" that can be compensated for by utilizing various Green Revolution technologies. Such approaches, they argue, reinforce the presumed superiority of first-world technologies (coupled with economic policies imposed by the World Bank) as the solution to third-world problems. Clearly, the circulation of culinary capital does not occur exclusively within a hermetically sealed culture but rather involves transnational and cross-cultural exchanges that often serve as springboards to power within one's home culture.

At the same time, just as culinary capital helps to determine the contours of transnational hierarchies, its contours too are shaped by global labor conditions, food supplies, and appropriated local knowledges. For example, as U.S. consumers find more and more items labeled "organic" on their supermarket shelves and as the culinary elite promotes such foods as healthy alternatives to industrially produced products, both the economic and symbolic value of organic foods increase as consumers pay significantly higher prices for both the products and the culinary capital that they confer. While contemporary food writers elevate organic farmers to celebrity status, however, others remind us that such farming methods are not their invention nor are they solely the purview of a new U.S.-based culinary elite. As the narrator of the Frontline/Nova documentary *Harvest of Fear* (2001) explains, "In Africa, virtually every farmer is an organic farmer. Here it's called subsistence agriculture." Even as Kenyan scientist Florence Wambugu argues that such farming methods cannot adequately produce enough food to feed her country, she acknowledges the "indigenous wisdom" that Kenyan farmers have utilized to keep their crops growing (*Harvest of Fear* 2001). Saying that Kenyan farmers are "very intelligent" even as she advocates modern technology and genetic modification as solutions for increasing productivity, Wambugu complicates a narrative that privileges the United States over developing nations based on its recent embrace of organic farming by the culinary elite (*Harvest of Fear* 2001). Ultimately, in order to fully appreciate how culinary capital circulates across the landscape of contemporary American culture, it is crucial to understand it as a transnational and cross-cultural phenomenon that gains added significance precisely at times when some nations face uncertainty about the production and distribution of food while other nations enjoy relative food security.

ANALYZING CULINARY CAPITAL IN ACTION

Each of the following chapters analyzes a site in American culture where making, watching, talking about, and consuming food is intricately connected to creating and sustaining an identity marked by status, power, and high levels of knowledge. Recognizing that "in modern times, people most often construct their own identities and define others through the commodities they purchase" (Halter 2000, 7), each chapter examines sites where the shaping of a culinarily capitalized self is facilitated by individual consumer practices. At the same time, it is important to recognize that the choices of individual consumers are made within a media-saturated environment that promotes specific food-related values and practices. In other words, because it is through consumption practices that we express "who we are," the modern marketplace benefits from generating and offering to feed a never-satiated demand for information about lifestyles (Featherstone 1991, 114). Consequently, these chapters focus on producer and consumer practices as a lens on culinary capital in each setting. We do not intend these as an exhaustive collection of sites for the workings of culinary capital, but rather a sampling of several of the most illuminating. In paying attention to these practices, we take care to avoid reading, and thus dismissing, consumption as merely a debased derivative of production, following the lead of Mike Featherstone (1991).

Chapter 2 examines meal assembly businesses and online grocery shopping. We explore the extent to which these new developments in food preparation and procurement disrupt and reproduce gender and class dichotomies within the context of our consumer-based economy. Accessible to the middle class, meal assembly businesses and e-grocers help consumers to crystallize a culinarily capitalized identity as they simultaneously respond to concerns about the harried pace of family life, resist oppressive gender constructions, and reinforce traditional ideas about family, health, and good citizenship. For individuals responsible for preparing fresh and healthy meals for their families but who find themselves challenged by the lack of time to do so, meal assembly businesses and e-grocers offer solutions that sustain rather than undermine their claim to culinary capital. Rather than abandoning family-oriented eating practices that revolve around fresh, home-cooked meals in favor of quick but "unhealthy" alternatives such as convenience, processed, or fast foods, individuals are invited to make "healthier" choices for themselves and their families in ways that accommodate the realities of contemporary time constraints. However, as these consumers rely on meal assembly businesses or e-grocers to procure fresh foods and prepare healthy, home-cooked meals, they may not recognize the ways in which these practices both depend upon and obscure certain class-based roles and relationships. Even as meal assembly businesses shift the traditionally invisible work done by women in the privacy of their home kitchens into the public sphere, they promote another kind of invisibility, namely, the work done by staff to prep for meal assembly sessions, clean up after them, maintain the facility, and prepare ready-to-cook meals for consumers who opt to buy them pre-packaged. Similarly, while e-grocers allow consumers to fulfill their duty of shopping for themselves and their families, they do so by relying on staff to receive, process, and deliver orders. In short, while meal assembly businesses and e-grocers allow middle-class consumers to continue seeing themselves as good citizens who "cook" and "shop" for their families, they do so by shifting much of the actual work to staff who remain largely invisible. This staff, primarily composed of workers of color, may derive more status from supporting aspirational performances of culinary capital than they do from preparing middlebrow food, although they remain economically exploited in relation to their white "front-of-house" counterparts (Jayaraman 2011). Dynamics like these make meal assembly businesses and e-grocers important, if problematic, tools for consumers in contemporary projects of the Self.

Chapter 3 explores the hugely popular phenomenon of television cooking shows as catalysts for projects of the Self. The chapter considers how cooking programming has evolved into its current varied forms as we use the frameworks of the self-help movement and reality television to understand how contemporary food programming circulates culinary capital. Focusing particularly on the Food Network, we examine how its history, evolution, and contemporary iterations reflect, rely on, circulate, and/or challenge normative ideologies of gender and class. Specifically, we review the breadth of the Food Network's programming, arguing that what connects these seemingly disparate formats is the network's desire to market itself to the largest possible audience by offering various models of good citizenship to the broadest spectrum of viewers. The network offers shows that are framed around traditional narratives of women who dedicate the bulk of their time to cooking for their families; shows that update this narrative as they market themselves to viewers who confront the challenge of meeting this obligation within the confines of limited time and/or money; others that highlight men in a space customarily occupied by women; and programs that shift the focus from cooking for pleasure to cooking as competition. While each of these programs makes implicit claims about the transformative power of cooking, they do so in ways that require interrogation. Like the meal assembly businesses and e-grocers that we discuss in chapter 2, these programs both rely upon and mask labor done by those who remain off camera, including staff who do most of the required prep and clean-up work. While the network's on-screen personalities demonstrate their culinary knowledge and skills—as well as the culinary capital that comes with them—they do so in ways that obscure the conditions that make this possible. Consequently, they circulate a model of good citizenship and a promise of culinary capital with which viewers are invited to identify as they make their own personal lifestyle choices. The network offers knowledge to viewers that may help them feel satisfied and accomplished—successful in the system—which acts as a panacea that keeps them from looking more critically at the troublesome gendering of domestic expectations and bravado performance. Ultimately, the network offers its viewers a range of fantasies that are difficult, if not impossible, to attain even as it markets its celebrity chefs' cookbooks and other accoutrements as necessary tools for such a quest. In the end, we argue that the Food Network is first and foremost a capitalist enterprise that offers its viewers a diverse menu of food-related programming aimed at feeding their appetite for culinary capital and inviting them to participate as active consumers across the culinary landscape.

Chapter 4 moves on to examine restaurant criticism as another medium through which culinary capital circulates, focusing specifically on the transition from its traditional, print-based format to its more recent online iterations. As meal assembly businesses, e-grocers, and Food Network programs contribute to a culinary landscape that relies upon but obscures certain class-based hierarchies, we investigate how sites like Chowhound, Citysearch, Yelp, and a bevy of others replace this paradigm with a more ostensibly "democratic" and "egalitarian" format. Insofar as they purport to allow anyone to play the role of armchair food critic by posting a review, these sites claim to escape a class-based elitism that privileges the expert over the mass consumer. However, we argue that while they do expose and potentially disrupt this dichotomy, they also create their own culinary hierarchies. These sites mask realities of time and resources that limit supposedly universal access to them as users establish their unique identities in relation to their online rivals. As "chowhounds" set themselves up against much-despised "foodies," much is at stake. By analyzing Chowhound's framing narrative as well as a series of exchanges between its users, we conclude that such interactive, more easily accessible new media centered on food—much like their televised counterparts—keep people more invested than ever in a professional culinary elite that remains ever just out of reach as they serve as new tools for the accumulation of culinary capital.

In chapter 5 we transition from sites that promise culinary capital to consumers who accept and seek to emulate privileged food practices to sites that at first glance seem to challenge such norms. Given contemporary mantras about healthy eating and good citizenship, in this chapter we are interested in how such expectations are resisted within specific contexts that invite—and even reward—excessive and unhealthy eating. Specifically, we begin with an analysis of consumer eating practices and attitudes at carnivals and state fairs, sites where mandates for healthy and restrained eating seem to be suspended, at least temporarily. Based on interviews that we conducted with consumers at several fairs, we conclude that the pleasure that consumers experience through such an escape does not motivate a broader rejection of middle-class values but ironically indicates a more long-term embrace of them. We then move on to discuss the rising popularity of competitive eating, asking how competitors and fans alike make sense of this "sport"—a contested designation that we discuss at length—in relation to the normative pull of "acceptable" food and foodways. Fans of professional competitive eaters Kobayashi or Joey Chestnut cannot be said to be on the fast track to culinary capitalization within the privileged field of "foodie" discourse, yet the ironic stance adopted by International Federation of Competitive Eating (IFOCE) enthusiasts suggests a more complicated interplay among culinary capital, pleasure, and knowingness than is immediately evident. We pursue this argument further in the final part of the chapter, which explores how "junk" food websites and blogs function to create communities of "junk foodies" who openly and unapologetically embrace their love of these treats unaffected by recrimination by the culinary elite. Such sites promote radically different dietary practices in their celebration of junk food; however, while they can be read as challenging food-based and class-based hierarchies, they ultimately deploy many of the same tactics as those sites that promote healthy and restrained eating practices. Even in the topsy-turvy world of competitive eating and the junk food blogosphere, culinary capital is there for the taking—but the taking involves an embrace of food practices and ideologies that fly in the face of privileged food discourse. This chapter ultimately illustrates that what constitutes culinary capital is entirely arbitrary, but that those with symbolic capital have the capacity to make their claims about reality stick.

In the conclusion, we pull together the common themes that connect our analyses of cultural sites that produce and circulate culinary capital by attending to current shifts across the culinary landscape that indicate a melding of privileged and non-privileged food practices. We argue that such hybridization signals the emergence of a model of culinary capital that moves beyond either reinforcing normative hierarchies or promoting alternative food practices that do little to disrupt them. Specifically, we examine recent trends in three important culinary spaces—restaurants, supermarkets, and food-related television programming—each of which exhibits a shift toward blurring the boundaries between privileged and resistant food practices and the identities they help to create. Speculating as to the long-term impact of such boundary crossings, we conclude that they offer more than merely a temporary and contained form of "culinary dissent," but rather point to a form of consumer citizenship through which individual and collective acts of eating shape how food choices are made and culinary capital circulates.

Taken collectively, these chapters make clear that the norms and practices through which culinary capital is acquired are not static; rather, while a particular set of values and ideologies may privilege certain food practices at a specific historical moment, alternative ways of thinking and eating are never far away. While their marginalization may suggest that they have little impact on the mainstream culinary landscape, they nonetheless offer their own path toward culinary capitalization. At the same time, this tension between privileged and aberrant food practices reveals the complex role of culinary capital in shaping and reshaping the conditions in which individuals make their own food choices. As they do so, they also utilize culinary capital to create and sustain identities that earn them status as good citizens within their communities.

–2–

Fixing Dinner/Fixing the Self: The Contradictions of New Trends in Food Procurement

Recent years have witnessed increased attention to food and foodways across contemporary American popular culture, evidenced by the countless hours of television and film, as well as books and blogs, devoted to the topic. However, this comes at a time when we are told that most households spend less time cooking (U.S. Energy Information Administration 2010) and that the much exalted "family meal" is quickly disappearing (Putnam 2000; Weinstein 2005). Businesses that allow new ways of procuring and preparing food in this larger context are, we argue, marketing access to culinary capital. Such capital aids consumer citizens in projecting a better, more discerning and caring self, one who fulfills familial obligations with panache despite the challenges of our fast-paced contemporary lives.

Given the role that food practices play in animating ideologies of gender and class, we must consider what is at stake with new options for how, where, and what we shop for, cook, and eventually eat. The businesses we explore in this chapter, meal assembly kitchens and e-grocers, are ideologically ambivalent. They offer sophisticated and forward-looking solutions to the perennial problem of how to get good food on the table and confer distinction upon consumers who take advantage of their services as they attempt to "do it all"—to keep up with demanding careers while keeping themselves and their families well fed. At the same time, these businesses congratulate consumers for their unquestioning acceptance of the expectations that women should be primarily responsible for such tasks, and they mask the labor of Others on which the consumer citizen's status depends. These businesses market themselves by acknowledging the more complicated conditions under which women attempt to do domestic work, and as such can be read as affirming their customers' professional status instead of elevating a more old-fashioned point of view where the domesticated mother who stays home and bakes cookies is adulated. However, in endorsing the "you can have it all" mystique, these businesses sacrifice any critical examination of our expectations about who does the unglamorous, behind-the-scenes work that keeps families humming along, and thus they perpetuate traditional ideologies of gender and class.

What e-grocers and meal assembly kitchens offer—assistance with domestic work around food provisioning, specifically food shopping and meal preparation—has long been considered "women's work," and has moved aggressively into the public sphere in recent years. Given capitalism's penchant for transforming or creating new industries in response to an ever-changing cultural landscape, it is not surprising that a range of such businesses have emerged during a time of substantial change in how the work of feeding the family is performed. The businesses we explore here respond directly to familiar refrains about the lack of time available to the contemporary American family, and more particularly the women in these families, to accomplish this task. In presenting alternatives aimed at alleviating this problem, they expose many of the ideological underpinnings of American society even as they offer culinary capital as both the reward for utilizing their services and the means of protecting the American family.

The private work of the domestic kitchen has crossed the public/private divide in a variety of ways; as a result, this once invisible and alienated domestic work becomes a visible commodity capable of creating and circulating culinary capital. The businesses that we discuss in this chapter blur the boundary between the public and private spheres but as they do so, they are not pioneers traversing a never-before-crossed frontier; rather, they expose the fact that domestic culinary work, even when done in the private home, crosses this divide but that such breaches are acceptable to the extent that they remain invisible. Traditionally, this was accomplished through provisioning, as outlined by sociologist Marjorie DeVault: "The work connects 'public' and 'private' realms, but since it is largely invisible, the connections go unnoticed. Instead, people do shopping, and use their purchases, to produce 'personal life' and thus, actually to construct the boundaries between home and market" (1991, 60). While such provisioning ensures that traditional culinary work actually reinforces the boundaries that it crosses, the businesses that we discuss in this chapter rupture these categories in more critical ways. However, we conclude that despite such disruptions, they can also be read as reinforcing many of the categories and identities that they initially seem to challenge and that they invoke culinary capital as they do so.

MEAL ASSEMBLY KITCHENS, E-GROCERS, AND THE ROAD TO CULINARY CAPITAL

Springing up in the early to mid-2000s, meal assembly franchises with names like Dream Dinners and Dinner by Design (hereafter DBD) offer their customers—usually women—"meal solutions" to a number of problems, including the time and stress of planning, preparing and shopping for meals, the stress and mess of meal preparation, the drudgery of solitary kitchen work, and the lack of quality and variety associated with unhealthy processed and fast food. By enumerating the actual labor involved in feeding the family, these businesses make visible and important the kind of work to which DeVault implores us to pay attention. DeVault notes the thoughtful mental work of planning, coordination, juggling, and strategizing involved in feeding a family, apart from simple physical tasks of say, pushing a cart through a grocery aisle or frying a burger (1991, 56). She asks us to resist the "pervasive trivialization" of this kind of labor, and businesses like DBD respond empathetically.

Like meal assembly kitchens, online grocery services have become increasingly popular in the last decade. Sites like FreshDirect, NetGrocer, and Peapod have staked their claim to a growing market. At the same time, many traditional grocery stores, recognizing this trend toward online shopping, have developed their own web presences. Many analysts believe that with continued improvements in technology and home delivery systems, online shopping in general, and e-grocers in particular, will experience continued growth. An article heralding the arrival of online grocery shopping in Joplin, Missouri, situates this local development within a broader national context:

> While e-grocery shopping is in its infancy across the country, industry research predicts that it will experience steady growth as consumers realize its value. A report from the Food Marketing Institute reports that 3.7 million people shopped online for groceries in 2005. According to the New York–based firm Jupiter Research, Americans bought $3.3 billion worth of groceries online in 2005, with grocery ranking as the fourth largest online shopping category. Jupiter Research reports that sales from e-groceries are expected to grow at a compound annual rate of 23 percent through 2010. (Stark 2007)

In fact, America's largest online retailer, Amazon, has entered the food business in two ways, offering nonperishable foods through Amazon.com and introducing AmazonFresh in the Seattle area. According to its website, "Although Amazon.com founded AmazonFresh, AmazonFresh operates as an independent grocery delivery business" and, presumably, serves as a testing ground for future expansion into this growing market.

Both meal assembly kitchens and e-grocers are the newest incarnations in a long history of attempts to solve the problem of housework by commercializing it. Both businesses market themselves by highlighting the appeal of shared labor and benefit ideologically from the movement of this labor to public, albeit commercial, space. In meal assembly kitchens, kitchen gnomes have done all the chopping ahead of time, and whisk away the dishes, bowls, and utensils for back-room cleanup; in e-grocery stores, an army of employees combs through warehouses to personally package orders, which are then delivered by any one of their fleet of drivers during the delivery window specified by the customer.[1]

DeVault inspires a question about these "gnomes": from what class substrate are those who do the food preparation that allows meal assembly clients to float in and assemble their entrees? And where is race in this equation? DeVault says that "rather than purchasing the labor of women of color directly, as domestic servants, affluent white women increasingly benefit from the labors of others less directly, and perhaps more comfortably because relations of oppression and privilege are less visible" (DeVault 1991, 201; see McCullen 2011 for more on the racialized fetishization of food production). Saru Jayaraman, cofounder of the Restaurant Opportunities Center United, notes that race-based economic exploitation of workers is pervasive in the food service sector (2011). Any culinary capital that these workers may gain by supporting the gastronomic aspirations of their primarily white, middle-class customers must be viewed in this context.

Meal assembly businesses are certainly not part of the tradition of co-operative or communal cooking adopted by social progressives, as their cost is too dear. In contrast, these businesses follow more in the tradition of cooked-food delivery services that offered not exactly takeout, but promised a more extensive arrangement that covered meals seven days a week and existed briefly between 1884 and 1927.[2] Meals prepared centrally were delivered to individual households, leaving householders only to order, eat, clean up the dishes, and pay the bill. But historian Ruth Schwartz Cowan (1983) suggests these businesses never became popular, with even the largest of them serving only about a hundred families; none at all made it through the Depression.[3]

These businesses also share some lineage with the community kitchens and dining clubs that existed from about 1884 through 1925, which allowed some women to both relieve other women of cooking duties and to add to their family income. By organizing neighborhood dining clubs and cooked food delivery services, they accomplished both ends. Relatively affluent families found these to provide a huge time savings (Hayden 1981, 209). "The neighborhood dining clubs combined cooperative purchasing of food with collective preparation and dining. They emphasized social innovation, while the food delivery services tended to be run by entrepreneurs on a commercial basis and to emphasize technological innovation. The delivery services were often more expensive to patronize" (Hayden 1981, 209–210). Dining clubs were run in co-op fashion where hired cooks worked alongside members, with everyone taking a shift or paying for a substitute, and ended up costing members less than they could cook for at home (Hayden 1981, 212). Nonetheless, these clubs were ill-fated because "if a housewife's labor was never timed or counted, then it was very difficult to persuade husbands, or the community at large, that kitchen workers should receive wages comparable to the wages of a valued 'professional' worker, or that experiments which placed a cash value on cooked meals should be continued" (Hayden 1981, 214). Whether or not meal assembly businesses, which do place cash value not only on food but on the labor of preparation and cleanup, will face a similar fate remains to be seen; we do see them in decline, but the decline is typically attributed to the inability of the public to comprehend what exactly the product is (Kuhn 2009), rather than on their subversive efforts to monetize "women's work." But one thing remains the same: just as parts of the United States in the late nineteenth and early twentieth centuries welcomed entrepreneurs who were committed to certain ideals of community life, both meal assembly businesses and e-grocers may be understood to succeed in the same places because of their symbolic and practical contributions to maintaining a traditional conception of family and their desire for culinary capital in doing so. By assisting consumers in fulfilling their responsibilities to their families in ways that also allow them to embrace the culinary trends and expectations that permeate the contemporary foodscape—home-cooked meals that are nutritious and may feature organic, local, and/or sustainable ingredients—meal assembly businesses and e-grocers help individuals to make food choices and engage in culinary practices that affirm their status as good citizens. We argue that these businesses support those consumers who view their culinary practices as an essential part of their individual, familial, and social identities insofar as they invite membership into their idealized status groups.

Making food choices to preserve one's family offers currency within these idealized status groups. Cowan argues that dining clubs failed not because of economic tough times but because "when the choices were available (and capital, if nothing else, has surely tossed up choices), the majority of people—whether rich or poor, owners or workers, male or female—chose to preserve in both the realm of symbol and the realm of fact, those activities that they deemed crucial to the creation and maintenance of family life" (1983, 149). Historically, many commercial alternatives to home cooking have failed because Americans see them as corrupting family life and family autonomy. As Alan Warde states, "While the ability to purchase goods or services is restricted by income, there are also powerful normative obstacles to seeking commercial solutions to the problems of domestic provisioning" (1997, 153). We are hesitant about paying for domestic assistance, noting the virtue in expressing care for people and the intrinsic satisfaction, however small, of household tasks like cooking (Warde 1997, 154). While "women and men appear to be selectively investing unpaid work time in the tasks that construct family life while spending less time in routine tasks, suggesting that the symbolic meaning of unpaid work may be shifting" (Sayer 2005, 285; see also Bugge and Almas 2006), we need to make sense of this selective investment in family life and to consider how meal assembly kitchens and e-grocers address audiences who attempt simultaneously to resist oppressive constructions of gender even as they invoke culinary capital in order to preserve symbolic notions of family. From this perspective, we must investigate these businesses to see how they attempt a workaround as they utilize culinary capital to link the salvation of family life with the search for a solution to the problem of housework.

In their marketing, e-grocers like FreshDirect (hereafter FD) emphasize three related themes: convenience, affordability, and quality. The consumer who takes advantage of these features of online grocery shopping earns culinary capital as she procures superior products without wasting money or time. She is thereby distinguished from her peers who fritter precious resources or settle for inferior food products for themselves and their families. In identifying itself as a "new way to shop for food," FD's website explains how it works: "We've hired New York's food experts, built the perfect environment for food and found the shortest distance from farms, dairies and fisheries to your table. We have all the irresistibly fresh food you could want, plus popular grocery brands for up to 25% less than supermarket prices and we bring it right to your door." Promising "higher quality at lower prices," FD explains how it cuts out the middlemen as it brings food directly to the home "so it's several days fresher and a lot less expensive when it gets to your table." In this rhetorical turn, shoppers who actually go to the store are almost parochial dupes who are content to pay steep prices for flaccid food. In contrast, the FD shopper has the savoir faire to do better. As the company's tagline goes, "Our food is fresh. Our customers are spoiled." Highlighting the cleanliness of its facilities and the high standards of its food experts, FD promises to deliver quality, nutritious food to "your family" while saving you time and money, addressing a customer who earns distinction by doing the right thing in the family context.

If this all sounds too good to be true, the website includes testimonials from satisfied customers that reinforce its central themes. The testimonials are presented as genuine, although of course, they have been curated by the FD corporate mothership for particular effect. Thus, we are less interested in the veracity of these testimonials than in what FD wishes to communicate about itself by including them. For Teresa from Forest Hills and Sandra from the Upper West Side, time is the great resource that FD offers. Teresa writes, "Thanks for being a terrific service that has allowed me to . . . spend less time running out for groceries and household products"; and Sandra explains, "There is nothing more valuable than time and you guys really save a lot of that for me." For Elaine from Tribeca, the flexibility that comes with online shopping is especially beneficial to her family: "FreshDirect has truly made a difference in our food purchasing. Ordering late at night is the key ingredient as it is the only time I can sit down and focus. (We have twin toddlers ruling our house right now.)" Others emphasize quality and price: Alvin from Brooklyn Heights shares, "FreshDirect is just great. The quality and price of meat, vegetables and fruits is outstanding." Similarly, Lilla from the Upper West Side adulates, "Finally New Yorkers are able to purchase quality food at fair prices! You have brought cooking back into my home—thanks!" Still other satisfied customers echo these themes while also highlighting health and nutrition as well as the benefits FD has had on their families. For example, Melinda from Rego Park writes: "Have lost 20 pounds so far eating fresh vegetables, fruit and fish that are difficult to find and gather after work and on the weekends in crummy NYC stores. FD takes the drudgery out of shopping in NYC. It's so easy. Detailed ingredients and nutrition information makes [sic] it easy to shop for my gluten-free, casein-free 5-year-old son." In short, as it saves time and money, offers convenience and high quality, and supports healthy and nutritious eating, FD markets itself as an essential tool for meeting the demands of the modern American family. It also it confers culinary capital upon those who embrace their responsibility for feeding their families nutritious, home-cooked meals in a cultural environment that makes this an increasingly difficult task to accomplish.

These themes also predominate in the marketing of meal assembly businesses. For example, the DBD website tells customers to "be ready for some fun," noting that when they arrive they'll "see all the hard work" that's been done that will allow them to "spend two hours or less enjoying the meal assembly process, socializing with others while putting together your entrées in easy to store, complimentary containers." With a wink and a nod, the business also notes that "if time is tight, the Dinner by Design staff will prepare your meals for you." This added level of service connects DBD with a growing trend in online grocery shopping, namely, increased emphasis on prepared or "ready-to-eat" meals. According to a short blurb in *Business Week*, "FreshDirect...reports it is seeing growth in areas such as ready-to-eat meals....To feed that demand, the company has been expanding its '4-minute meals' line of entrees, developed in conjunction with upscale eateries such as Rosa Mexicana and Tabla" (McConnon 2008, 16). This is particularly interesting, in that both meal assembly kitchens and e-grocers set themselves up against the fast or processed food to which busy families often resort, many of which themselves have mutated to require home cooks to add fresh ingredients to packaged foods in an overture to mothers who recognize the importance of performing the work of care. A Kraft spokesperson told *New Products Magazine*, "Although moms don't want to spend time shopping or chopping, they do want some involvement with the meal preparation to feel they are providing a fresh and home-cooked meal for their families" (Dahm, cited in Glassner 2007, 86).

This is precisely what FD offers through its "4-minute meals," "ready to cook," and "heat & eat" options. The first of these options invites customers to "enjoy portability, speed and convenience without giving up flavor or fresh-ness," assuring them that all they need is "four minutes and a microwave!" The second option, "ready to cook," explains to customers that they can "save time and get a head start on home-cooked meals with an array of deli-cious prepared dining options that are ready to go straight to your grill, oven or stovetop." Here, home cooks looking to save time can also find "essential cook's helpers like peeled garlic, handmade stocks and marinades." The third option, "heat & eat," offers "easy, delicious meals," explaining that "chef Mi-chael Stark (formerly of Tribeca Grill) and his team prepare a menu of easy lunch options and delicious, ready-to-heat meals" that "bring you real food, real fast. Just heat and enjoy!" In each case, FD, like DBD, offers moms the convenience of fresh and nutritious meals in ready-to-eat formats that still allows them an admittedly limited role in their preparation. In doing so, they enable the conferral of culinary capital upon those women who seek strat-egies for fulfilling their traditional domestic duties inasmuch as these meals do require *some* cooking, even if the realities of contemporary American cul-ture provide them with diminishing time for doing so. Bonus culinary capital goes to those shoppers who pick their fresh ready-to-heat meals from trendy DBD storefronts or stores with a cult following like Trader Joe's or Whole Foods, or have them delivered by the au courant FD. These vendors possess a certain degree of cachet that positively inflects, by association, what one pur-chases there, in contrast, for example, to a frozen Swanson dinner purchased in the food section of one's local Wal-Mart. Regardless of provenance, though, such convenience products have been vilified by the Center for Science in the Public Interest, labeled "food porn" and derided for their speed, convenience, and fattiness (Glassner 2007, 86–87).

In a parallel to our focus on meal assembly kitchens and e-grocers, Joe Moran contrasts frozen meals "meant for poorer shoppers looking for special offers" with chilled meals, "a virtual middle-class monopoly," like those high-lighted by FD's "4-minute meal," "ready to cook," and "heat & eat" options. "Today, convenience food is the focus of disparate anxieties about farm mech-anization, unhealthy additives, the dangers of obesity and the dominance of the big retailers. The chilled ready meal avoids these associations through its implicit links with a particular class identity: the 'cash-rich, time-poor' pro-fessional" (Moran 2005). Moran claims that middle-class consumers like to think they're doing something active: "We have invented an activity some-where between microwave instantaneity and cooking from scratch: food as-sembly" (2005). Similarly, Warde notes that "all cookery is of this nature; labour is added, and by transforming groceries into meals social and symbolic value is created" (Warde 1997, 152; see also Neuhaus 1999 for more on the imperative to tweak and personalize convenience food). This logic is further extended by both meal assembly businesses and e-grocers as they diminish the labor required to manipulate the groceries for the transformative effect of social and symbolic value, that is, culinary capital.

GENDER, STATUS, AND THE LABOR OF CARE

The extent to which both DBD and FD emphasize helping women to continue taking an active role in feeding their families suggests that they may be read as using the promise of culinary capital to affirm a particular gender ideology as they assist women in making choices that align with their traditional roles. DBD addresses women directly, though slyly, using gendered images rather than gendered verbal appeals: the headline banner on the DBD homepage shows a conventional nuclear family seated at dinner, with only the adult woman swiveled around facing the camera, and the caption: "Make time for you." Likewise, all three photos of the meal preparation sessions that are included depict only women cooking or close-ups on women's hands holding DBD packages. Men are noticeably absent, and when they are portrayed, it is in the background as eaters of the meal, rather than as preparers. FD carefully avoids any verbal mention of the gender of its intended market segment, and displays only photos of food on its main web pages, in what is likely a deliberate bid to cast the widest possible net for customers. However, its video testimonials, nicely strung together in a polished segment called "What Our Customers Are Saying," depict four customers, three of whom are women. These three are coded in dress and milieu quite differently: one is "professional," one is "edgy/artsy," and one is a "mom with twins." Both the professional woman and the mom refer to their families in their testimonials, with the professional expressing gratitude that FD allows her to make good choices for her family, and the mother articulating relief that she doesn't have to drag her infant twins to the store with her to shop. But even apart from this direct mode of customer address, FD's stress on "feeding your family" no doubt speaks to women, who have been historically saddled with this task.

Even though the FD videos distinguish the "professional" woman from the "mom," rather than forcing women to choose between a professional career outside of the home and their traditional duties within it, these businesses support women's desires to balance the two. They promote themselves as helping women to sustain their identities as good wives and mothers who make healthy and nutritious food choices for their families rather than resorting to unhealthy choices—fast food or processed, industrially produced, frozen food—to make up for ever-increasing and often conflicting demands on their time and energy, a phenomenon elaborated on by John Thompson (2011). However, while meal assembly businesses claim to take the work of shopping and planning that goes with feeding the family entirely off a woman's shoulders, the reality is otherwise, given the need to think about menus ahead of time, to balance family needs and preferences, to drive to and from the business, and to spend hours there prepping the meals. In addition, there is the fact that most meal assembly businesses offer only entrée assembly, thus requiring more preparation of accompanying dishes at home.[4]

Despite these limitations, however, meal assembly businesses do create spaces in which women's labor becomes visible. Betty Friedan (1963) woke us, half a century ago, from any delusions about the extent to which wives and mothers toiling alone in kitchens to feed the family are considered heroic; instead, they are invisible and alienated, and in the contemporary context of two-income families, it is unlikely that they "read" as culinarily capitalized.[5] Women don't get paid in dollars at a meal assembly business—there are no wages forthcoming at the end of a dinner prep session—but they do find themselves enriched in terms of culinary capital. Another part of the promise of meal assembly kitchens and e-grocers has to do with their situation in space. Numerous feminist critics have argued that the traditional insularity of the domestic kitchen bodes well neither for the work that happens within it nor for the possibility of social structural change in economics and gender relations. Heidi Hartmann contends that only "changing boundaries between home and market production" may result in decreased housework, as "production formerly done by women at home may be increasingly shifted to capitalist production sites" (1981, 389). Of course, both meal assembly businesses and e-grocers still involve work on the part of women; in the former, prepping and cleaning up are simply replaced by driving (Warde 1997, 127), and in the latter, the physical trip to the grocery store is replaced by a virtual one. Additionally, it is presumable that time saved through these services is often redirected to other forms of unpaid labor.

More compelling are arguments that locate the transformative potential of non-insular enterprises. While e-grocers may be seen as *more* insular insofar as they eliminate one opportunity for domestic culinary work to move physically into the public sphere via the trip to the supermarket, recall DeVault's notion of provisioning: "people do shopping, and use their purchases, to produce 'personal life' and thus, actually to construct the boundaries between home and market" (1991, 60). To what extent does the transformation of the shopping experience into a virtual one disrupt such provisioning and the gendered identities that it supports? Does the merger of the supermarket and computer technology shift the gender dynamics of virtual grocery shopping? Similarly, can meal assembly businesses be read as a reply to the materialist feminists' critique of the home as a cut-off domestic workplace (Gilman 1898; Hayden 1981, 295), inasmuch as they bring domestic workers together in non-domestic settings?

Perhaps more important than the fact that meal assembly kitchens and e-grocers move domestic culinary work into a quasi-public physical or virtual environment is what happens in these spaces: namely, how do users of meal assembly businesses and e-grocers use these spaces? Do they constitute places where we rethink our presumptions about the "mundane" and "un-skilled" work of domestic cookery (Floyd 2004, 62)? Writing in a different context, geographer Janet Floyd refers to cooking programs that feature pro-fessional chefs in kitchen contexts that seem a little homey but are devoid of familial interruptions, but that also aren't fully "professional" in the sense of hierarchies and gleaming steel, suggesting that such shows "rewrite the kitchen as a space in which the cook performs independently and manages a series of tasks, simple as well as complex, without recourse to any respon-sibility or authority" (Floyd 2004, 64). In this context, it is interesting to note how FD functions as a virtual space that blurs this distinction between the home cook and the professional chef, especially as it offers meals designed in collaboration with trendy New York restaurants or that have been created by their own resident expert chefs. In this way, FD offers its customers another means of acquiring culinary capital as they bring designer meals from the hot-test new chefs and restaurants to their kitchen tables (akin to our discussion in chapter 4 of the role of culinary elitism in identity formation). Whether the same can be said of the meaning of work at meal assembly businesses re-quires an investigation of autonomy and agency in those spaces.

While both meal assembly kitchens and e-grocers shift the physical and virtual spaces in which domestic culinary work is performed, they do not dis-rupt fully the economic and ideological structures through which it has been framed and to which it makes an important contribution. Meal preparation as a component of housework is characterized by the absence of the clear stan-dards and direct management typical of paid labor. But while cooking has, for some women, exceptional status as a rewarding and creative form of house-work (Gussow 1987, 42), the ambiguity of domestic culinary standards and the nebulous ways in which discursive ideals of family life nonetheless de-mand acquiescence may leave women anxious and self-doubting about their ability to feed their families appropriately. Alan Warde points out that in con-trast to chores for which little experience and knowledge is needed, but for which much elbow-grease is required, "cooking is creative" and it "involves knowledge and practical skill" (1997, 147). As such, middle-class and profes-sional women, with their long formal educational histories and their frequent isolation from their own families of origin, are quite receptive to this expert advice (DeVault 1991, 221; Rose 1999, 74). It is in these situations where external authorities like DBD and FD step in to lend a hand, allowing women to maintain the autonomy that domestic workers cite as a pleasurable aspect of their work, to assuage possible anxieties about their inadequacy as good caretakers, and to claim their share of culinary capital in the process.[6]

One might question whether different norms of class and gender are performed in households that are similar in terms of aspirational socioeconomic status, but inflected by non-normative status in terms of race or sexuality of family members. The act of feeding the family creates family in hetero homes as well as LGBT ones, black and white alike. It is this feeding work that creates class identities as well as gender, ethnic, racial, and sexual identities. In a study of lesbian and gay households, Christopher Carrington notes that affluent and aspirational lesbigay families value novelty, exoticness, and healthfulness (2008, 267), just like their hetero counterparts of the same class status. They also make distinctions between the person who does the cooking in the household versus the person who does the shopping and cleaning, in an effort to demonstrate egalitarianism, but Carrington contends that the majority of the labor of provisioning in lesbigay families is really performed by the cook (2008, 265). It is easy to see how meal assembly businesses and e-grocers would be appealing in this context, helping a lesbian or gay partner to relieve the burden of provisioning. Carrington's contention that "purchasing feeding work in the marketplace enables more affluent [lesbigay] couples to achieve a greater degree of egalitarianism in their relationships" (2008, 282) clearly explains that the allure of these services is not limited to normative hetero families.

Likewise, in her study of gender, food, and identities in her own African American/Ghanaian household, Psyche Williams-Forson explains how she and her husband came to rely upon the cooking of her sisters-in-law as well as an underground network of women illegally selling Ghanaian food in order to satisfy her husband's appetites and to allow her to prioritize her professional life over her provisioning duties. When she writes that "primary food providers engage in survivalist techniques and strategies that assist in humanizing multiple environments" (Williams-Forson 2012, 148), she could just as well be talking about meal assembly businesses or e-grocers. In all of these cases, consumers rely on the extra labor of (usually underpaid) others in order to satisfy their own desires and to perform particular identities. Thus, normative white families are not alone in their reliance on the marketplace to support their provisioning efforts.

Another important aspect of domestic culinary work, according to Warde, is the extent to which it can be constructed as a form of gift-giving (1997, 147). Meal assembly businesses preserve the semblance of creativity and skill, though their sessions are highly prescriptive in a paint-by-numbers way, while also emphasizing gift-giving as the logic that frames women's unpaid contributions to the family (Coontz 1992, 54–67). However, as men's traditional role as breadwinner has eroded, it makes less sense to read women as using food merely to express their appreciation for that breadwinning (Kemmer 2000, 328). Similarly, e-grocers, by providing necessary resources in a timely and convenient way, allow women to demonstrate and expand their culinary knowledge and skills and to maintain their role in this gift economy. So what exactly are the "gifts" that meal assembly businesses and e-grocers give, and to whom are they given? The gifts appear to be time and convenience for the cook, quality nutritious food for the family members who later eat it, and culinary capital to the family that protects traditional narratives around cooking and eating and the ideologies of gender and class that they promote.

CLASS AND THE ALLURE OF PACKAGED CARE

As much as these sites might facilitate participation in a "gift economy," it is a gift with a considerable price. Meal assembly customers certainly aren't there for the financial savings: although the DBD website maintains that each serving works out to around four dollars, "which is less than most fast food options and much more nutritious," they fail to mention that this math takes into account only the entrée (usually meat or poultry), and none of the side dishes that would normally be considered to make a meal complete in an American household (Douglas 1999).[7] Similarly, while FD claims to offer "popular grocery brands for up to 25% less than supermarket prices," its "4-minute meals," "ready to cook," and "heat & eat" options are significantly higher priced. In DeVault's study, more affluent women spoke about economizing as a voluntary activity, often balancing money with the more scarce commodity in their lives, time (1991, 175)—a position that jibes with the "time saving" rhetoric of both DBD and FD; virtue and status (i.e., culinary capital) come not from financial sacrifice, but from taking time (but not too much!) out of one's already busy day to do things right for one's family—which comes at a financial cost. Thus affluence helps some to culinarily capitalize in ways that remain out of reach for more financially compromised people. DeVault suggests that a simple, ideological model of consumer behavior fails to pay attention to structural factors that make access to "choices" widely variable. Discourse that emphasizes the image of the "smart shopper," a class-less smartie who virtuously balances cost and need to provide for her family, "obscures crucial differences in the work of provisioning and in the different kinds of 'family' people are able to produce" (DeVault 1991, 201).

In fact, while offering a range of services aimed at allowing women to maintain their gendered identities as wives and mothers responsible for nourishing their families and infusing such identities with culinary capital in a society in which their legitimacy has been challenged, meal assembly kitchens and e-grocers make few overt gestures toward class. While FD does emphasize affordability in its marketing, its demographic is clearly the middle and upper-middle classes. Similarly, the seemingly classless "mother" and "family" to whom DBD markets itself is solidly middle class. This is apparent when DBD's marketing suggests that those who eat fast food or processed food, presumably lower-class families, are not, in fact, sharing family dinners even when they do so together. To protect time-crunched middle-class families from resorting to such options for feeding themselves, DBD markets itself as the preferred option for such families, contending that family dinner time is absolutely vital for a number of reasons. Vaguely citing scholarly research and popular publications, the DBD website notes that family dinners are associated with happier marriages, stronger family ties, and healthier, less overweight, more socially skilled, less behaviorally troubled, less drug-addicted children. While FD does not make such claims overtly, these same themes emerge in the customer testimonials. However, scholar Anne Murcott questions the evidentiary basis for the claim that family meals are in decline, noting the class bias of such a claim, with upper middle-class women placing heavy emphasis on the centrality of the family meal in stark contrast to working-class women "who still value the family, but accord the meal comparatively little significance as a symbol of it" (1997, 40). Furthermore, the rhetorical linkage of fast and processed food to the absence of family dinners helps to moralize the DBD experience in its emphasis on avoiding harm to children (Rozin 1997, 392). DBD argues on their homepage that "nationally, the time pressures at home and a steady decline in family dinner time means that families are sacrificing nutrition for the quick fix of fast food, leading to a dramatic increase in cases of childhood obesity," invoking the sine qua non of all current moral panics to make the case for the necessity of the service they offer. It is not enough to save time; apparently, one has to save the children from the adipose menace as well. Recall FD customer Melinda, who lost twenty pounds eating fresh vegetables, fruit, and fish, and had a much easier time shopping for her gluten-free, casein-free five-year-old son. It is precisely *this* kind of heroic effort on behalf of the family, undertaken in the public space of the meal assembly kitchen or the virtual space of the online grocery store, that secures culinary capital—a battle very much in keeping with Marjorie DeVault's findings about the cultural emphasis on the gravity of women's maternal responsibilities for children (1991, 114).

Ultimately, while we can read the transformations in how domestic culinary work is done as revealing and even challenging ideologies of gender and class, they simultaneously expose the fact that part of the appeal of businesses like meal assembly kitchens and e-grocers is rooted in their ability to utilize culinary capital in the process of identity-making in the context of late capitalism. As such, they echo our discussion in chapter 1 as they promote food choices and culinary practices that support normative discourses around healthy bodies, healthy families, and, by extension, healthy citizens. At the same time, they confer status on patrons who rely on their services— and the culinary capital that comes with them—to sustain their own sense of self. Such consumers eschew mass-produced commodities as signifiers of who they are, since they are all too easy to come by, and their proliferation ultimately renders their meanings ambiguous. Instead, they tweak. They buy mass-produced products and then adapt them to their own needs and desires in order to represent who they are individually or collectively, no longer caring that the commodity was mass-produced in the first place.

In short, these businesses promise culinary capital to those who embrace ideologies of gender and class in ways that ensure a healthy and disciplined citizenry, including the idealized wife and mother who stimulates the economy, cares for her family, and upholds nutritional discourses all in one fell swoop. John Coveney notes that nutrition has become "on the one hand, part of the duty to be well, and, on the other, part of the 'good' child, the 'good' parent and the 'good' citizen"—both a physical and spiritual discipline (Coveney 2000, 176). Nutrition is governance via food choice that allows individuals to produce themselves as ethical subjects and good citizens. Inasmuch as meal assembly businesses and e-grocers invoke discourses of nutrition in selling their products, they offer consumers the chance to make good choices for themselves and their families while earning their share of culinary capital in the process. Participating in a meal assembly session or making healthy selections from the myriad products available at the e-grocer is not, after all, a requirement. Instead, it is a choice, part of what Nikolas Rose describes as "a web of visibilities, of public codes and private embarrassments over personal conduct: we might term this *government through the calculated administration of shame*. Shame here was to entail an anxiety over the exterior deportment of the self, linked to an injunction to care for oneself in the name of the public manifestation of moral character. These strategies govern all the more effectively because each individual is to play his or her part in the games of civility" (Rose 1999, 73).

The very nature of the meal assembly kitchen requires that the private choices made by presumably free individuals about what to feed one's family are made public as one places one's order in advance of the session and prepares these meals in the company of other preppers and under the watchful eye of expert staff. Similarly, e-grocers engage in practices that blur the distinction between presumably private choices and the public manipulation of them. One feature of the online grocery shopping experience that is heralded as making a significant contribution to its ease and convenience is the personal profile. In creating such profiles, shoppers not only store basic information including name, address, payment method, and delivery preferences to facilitate their shopping experience, they also create "shopping lists" that

record and store their purchases. These lists can be retrieved and repli-
cated in future shopping sessions as a means of streamlining the selection
process. However, these personal shopping lists are not exclusively private
documents; rather, they provide essential data to e-grocers about consumer
habits, trends, and preferences.

Several e-grocers have also begun to use this information to recommend
products to customers based on their past purchases. It is no longer just the
person at the supermarket check-out counter who knows what food choices
you are making for yourself and your family. While e-grocers allow for the
physical relocation of the shopping experience from public supermarkets to
the privacy of the home, they simultaneously remind consumers that their
choices—even those made via the Internet—are not entirely private. With
e-grocers using personal shopping lists to track selections, compile data, anticipate behavior, and influence future choices, consumers are more likely to
engage in a form of self-monitoring that may cause them to compromise their
freedom of choice in order to conform to dietary norms and expectations as
these presumably private choices become increasingly public knowledge, a
concern that is echoed in the broader debate about privacy on the Internet
(Levmore and Nussbaum 2011). The reward for adapting one's behavior to
reflect privileged food discourses, however, is culinary capital and the status
group identification that comes with it.

Such self-policing could be taken to a new level as yet another Internet-
based technology enters the home and, like the personal computer, facilitates
a further erosion of the boundary between the private and public spheres.
This new technology for streamlining the grocery shopping experience is the
Ikan, a device whose very name bespeaks individual agency: "I can!" This
new appliance, which could "eliminate trips to the grocery store," is essentially a "bar code scanner...mounted on a countertop stand, an undercabi-
net bracket or a wall mount" with "a laser scanner...and a Wi-Fi antenna." It
works like this: "Each time you're about to throw away an empty container—for
ketchup, cereal, pickles, milk, macaroni, paper towels, dog food or whatever—
you just pass its bar code under the scanner. With amazing speed and ac-
curacy, the Ikan beeps, consults its online database of one million products,
and displays the full name and description. In a clear, friendly font, the screen
might say: 'Nabisco Reduced Fat Ritz Crackers 14.5 Oz.' for example. Now
you can toss the box, content that its replacement has been added to your
shopping list. After a few days of this, you can review the list online at Ikan.
net—and if everything looks good, click once to have everything delivered to
your house at a time you specify" (Pogue 2008, C1).

While David Pogue, in his *New York Times* article about the Ikan, emphasized both its environmental benefits and time-saving potential, we cannot
overlook its ability to bring Big Brother directly into our kitchen, recording not

only what we buy, but what we eat, when we eat it, and whether or not we are going to replace it! Is it farfetched to envision a day when we hide guilty pleasures, tossing empty Häagen-Dazs cartons directly into the trash while scanning uneaten containers of fat-free yogurt in order to create a much healthier e-profile and escape the wrath of our Ikan?

By making personal food choices available for public scrutiny, meal assembly kitchens and e-grocers (and soon the Ikan) offer opportunities for the enactment of citizenship not in relation to the state or a singular public sphere; instead, these options blend the private, the corporate, and the quasi-public (Rose 1999, 166). In doing so, they stave off the shaming of women who fail to fulfill traditional roles in relation to their families, enabling access to culinary capital as they reproduce discourses of family dependent on expert knowledges that imagine prepped meals and healthy food choices as constitutive of proper parenting. But Bugge and Almas extend the argument to point out that "cooking is not something urban middle-class women do only to produce home and family, but also to place themselves in the class hierarchy" (2006, 212). DeVault has noted that because familial gender positions—wife, mother, husband, father—seem to be irrelevant to class, they trickily mask the class differences they help to produce (1991). As such, we need to be sensitive to the ways in which seemingly unmarked performances of femininity or motherhood can be read in relation to discourses about social class, including Bourdieu's work on status group identities that are created and sustained through consumption patterns and lifestyle practices (see Bourdieu 1985).

Given the economic realities of meal assembly kitchens and e-grocers, it is apparent that they are largely middle-class phenomena. While working-class individuals tend to focus on tradition and convention in describing their foodways, professional/middle-class people exalt the values of novelty, experimentation, and presentation (DeVault 1991, 211). (To this list we would add healthiness.) In this paradigm, e-grocers can be situated within the context of a broader cultural shift into a virtual economy, one that by its very nature presumes a certain level of economic and cultural capital. Similarly, meal assembly can be a pleasurable and entertaining novelty in its own right rather than a means to an end—a point underscored by DBD franchise owners who, in an interview, described their kitchen as a kind of party space for fun and relaxation by "groups of girlfriends who bring wine and chat and laugh" and families who enjoy the change of scenery. Part of the reward here is also, surely, the mutual admiration among culinarily capitalized meal assemblers and savvy e-shoppers. Whereas Arlene Kaplan Daniels notes a lack of attention to and respect for work done in the home/private sphere (1987, 406), work done in meal assembly kitchens garners validation, particularly for women who take time out of their busy schedules to cook for their families.

Groups and individual preppers interact with one another, complimenting each other on technique and choice of entrée, among other things.

However much the assembly sessions may provide an opportunity for conversation and adulation, they are in decline, particularly on the East Coast, where one franchise owner has seen meal assembly sessions dwindle to only 5 percent of his business (Carnall 2009). Founded in the United States in 2002, the number of such enterprises grew steadily and peaked in 2007 with 1,353 outlets nationwide; however, by 2010, that number had dropped to 867, suggesting a quite rapid demise (Kuhn 2009). The group sessions have been edged out by the "grab and go" option, where interaction is limited to the check-out transaction (Carnall 2009) and where the result is very similar to shopping in the prepared-foods aisle of a regular grocery store or ordering the ready-to-eat options from an e-grocer. However, not all "grab and go" options are created equal, reminds one independent operator of Chicagoland meal assembly business, Entrees By You: "Cooking your meal fresh at home instead of just reheating an already-cooked meal ensures its freshness and will not compromise its quality. It's a different niche than reheating a Boston Market dinner" (Kuhn 2009). In this configuration, being the *original* heater of a premade meal is a mark of distinction that sets one apart from the frozen dinner/reheating crowd.

Frequently, convenience foods have been pitched as women's liberation from kitchen drudgery—and thus efforts to critique them are rebuffed as playing into the hands of those who would keep women suffering in domestic isolation (Gussow 1987, 39). Meal assembly businesses represent convenience when compared with cooking from scratch, but are certainly far less convenient than take-out, prepackaged foods, or fast food, given the necessary investment of time on-site to assemble the meal and at home to actually cook. Similarly, e-grocers do offer a range of conveniences when compared to trekking to the local supermarket, but they can also be read as exacerbating the trend toward a 24-hour cycle of work that is made more feasible by modern technology. Recall Elaine from Tribeca, who does her ordering late at night after attending to her twin toddlers all day. Feminist critics like Joan Dye Gussow might imagine meal assembly businesses and e-grocers as artifacts of the mandate that food industries grow, suggesting that they induce overconsumption, buying less food value for more money. Gussow, borrowing from the work of Mary Anselmino, argues that despite women's convictions in the early part of twentieth century that cooking was pleasurable and rewarding, a site for creativity, women's media actively worked to erode this positive regard in order to ensure industry growth. "Growth is achieved by creating food innovations that housewives and other working women must be convinced they need. This means that we as women must decide whether we want and need these food objects on some basis other than a belief that they have been made for our benefit and will ultimately save us time" (Gussow 1987, 43). Ultimately, we conclude that women who embrace these new businesses find this alternative motivation in the promise of culinary capital as a vehicle for identity formation and a marker of social status. At the same time, it is important to recognize that while meal assembly businesses and e-grocers have, of course, been established to make money and might not actually save that much time in the long run, they do arguably allow us to keep the pleasurable aspects of cooking while diminishing its less pleasant parts.

Rather than resorting to the stance that an appreciation for the convenient aspects of these businesses evidences false consciousness, we would do well to heed Gussow's call that we decide for ourselves whether they are valuable. Insofar as they promise culinary capital to sustain hegemonic ideologies of class and gender, meal assembly businesses and e-grocers function like other sources of culinary capital that we discuss in chapters 3 and 4. As they rely upon familiar themes of family, health, and good citizenship to promote themselves and their services, we must recognize their promise of culinary capital in ways that should not be read as socially transformative. While they may not demonstrate the kind of repressive power that forces women into a purely domestic role within the private sphere of the family, they do represent productive power as their patrons embrace their services as a means for creating and sustaining the culinarily capitalized identities that come with them. The self is remade as culinary capital functions as a blue ribbon for individual success that discourages more widespread agitation for real change. The culinary capital that these businesses offer has complicated moorings: as it progressively surfaces women's labor in the public realm, it simultaneously erases blue-collar labor. What this exploration proves is that we must avoid generalizations about how culinary capital functions in American culture in favor of contextualized analyses of its multifaceted, and often contradictory, meanings across our cultural and culinary landscape.

Television Cooking Shows: Gender, Class, and the Illusory Promise of Transformation

Together, we watch more than our fair share of food-related television, and we notice that it offers a variety of ways of being in relation to food that might be thought to increase one's social standing. The wide range of series offerings means that there is no single privileged way to be a good citizen in food TV world, but three possible paths emerge from our readings of this type of programming. First, one can be a kind of domestic goddess, fully inhabiting the home and feeding others extremely well. Second, one might be less of a regular in the kitchen, but when there, know how to healthfully provide for one's family and oneself with quality food while saving time and money. Third, one can vanquish obstacles to triumph over a challenge as one creates quality food. Indeed, the audience for cookery programs is diverse and encompasses seeming opposites, from "food activists (including 'healthy', 'local', 'sustainable', or 'organic' eaters) to those who delight in thumbing their noses at the so-called food police" (Rousseau 2012, x). To be rewarded, it seems enough merely to embrace the appeal and righteousness of one or more of these paths, rather than to follow it oneself by actually cooking anything. Television provides the basis of knowledge about these paths to good citizenship, producing the possibility that viewers can imagine themselves basking in the culinary capital of a Nigella Lawson, or a Paula Deen, or even a Bobby Flay, and thus find ways to distinguish themselves from the hoi polloi who, with their rushed fast food habits and their woeful ignorance of quality, are unmistakably inferior.

Indeed, as our society's dominant cultural storyteller, television provides "a coherent picture of what exists, what is important, what is related to what, and what is right" (Gerbner and Gross 1976, 76). While televised food programming dates back to the very beginnings of the medium, it has enjoyed unparalleled growth and expansion in recent years. The breadth and depth of contemporary food programming, evidenced by the success of the Food Network and its recent spinoff, the Cooking Channel, exemplifies the broader circulation of culinary capital across our cultural landscape. Like the meal assembly kitchens and e-grocers that we discussed in the previous chapter, the popularity of food-related programming signals an important shift in the visibility of food and food practices across the public terrain of American popular culture. At the same time, our examination of the sophisticated ways in which contemporary food programming has evolved exposes another important similarity among these phenomena, namely that each of them offers consumers a means of earning culinary capital through credible performances of a range of gender and class ideologies.

At the same time, it is important to note that among the many food series on television today, very few feature people of color in primary roles. When non-white individuals do appear, it is often in a nod toward cultural and culinary Otherness that both acknowledges difference and situates it in relation to normative white culture. However, the relative whiteness of this foodscape does not preclude identification by audience members of color, but it certainly doesn't go out of its way to encourage it, either. The predominant absence of racialized discourses in food television is suggestive about food, status, and power in non-normative (non-white) cuisines; they seem to matter relatively little, unless they inform mediated patterns of lowbrow "authentic" or rustic eating, or consumption of the exotic.

While food-related programs have emerged across the U.S. and international television landscape, from Bravo's wildly successful *Top Chef* to a growing roster of shows on the Travel Channel, this chapter focuses specifically on the U.S.-based Food Network, from its inception to its ongoing efforts to develop programming that draws an audience and fulfills the network's stated mission, which is broadening its viewer base while keeping roughly centered around the idea of food as consumer spectacle. As Toby Miller has noted, "Food TV is a key site of risk and moral panic, a space that physically forms and maintains citizens, gives them pleasure, and makes them vulnerable" (2007, 121). Our intent here is to explore how such programming promises its viewers access to culinary capital and, presumably, the personal and social transformations that come with it.

To organize our analysis of particular Food Network programs, we divide them into three broad categories: traditional, modern, and competitive. While such categorization is never absolute, it provides a useful framework for comparing and contrasting the different formats through which culinary capital circulates as it sustains ideologies of gender and class across a changing cultural landscape. By "traditional" programming, we mean those shows that are most closely related to the types of instructional cooking programs that emerged in the 1940s and 1950s—from the current roster of Food Network programs, we would include shows like *Ask Aida*, *Barefoot Contessa*, *Everyday Italian*, *Giada at Home*, *Nigella Feasts*, and *Paula's Home Cooking*. Such programs invite viewers to acquire culinary capital by embracing the kitchen as the space in which they can create and affirm their identities. While each of these shows has its own unique style, they share a direct lineage with a "classic" form of instructional food programming. Like Julia Child, who invited her viewers to learn the fundamentals of cooking as a necessary credential for meeting their familial and social roles (see DeVault 1991 for more on this gendered phenomenon), the hosts of these programs offer the acquisition of cooking skills—and the culinary capital that comes with this knowledge—as a means of securing one's social position by embracing various assumptions about class and gender.[1] To better understand how these programs utilize a well-established framework to promote traditional narratives about cooking, gender, and class, we contrast two very popular Food Network personalities, Paula Deen and Giada De Laurentiis. In doing so, we argue that while these two women and the shows that they host are quite different, what they share in common is a very traditional emphasis on women's identification with home and family while alluding to economic class only insofar as it promotes the myth of the transformative power of culinary capital. This genre offers viewers a mode of domestic, nurturing femininity that, if embraced, promises to produce a sense of distinction, as viewers are applauded for the culinary work they do to care for others around them.

While De Laurentiis's *Everyday Italian* makes gestures toward updating traditional dishes and techniques, this transition is realized more fully in programs that we categorize as "modern." Such shows combine a conventional understanding of women's domestic role with an acknowledgement that women are much less likely to be able to fully devote their time and energy to playing this role. At the same time, several recent additions to the Food Network roster make overt gestures to class by pitching themselves to viewers who may be feeling the crunch of the economic downturn and may need to prioritize economizing in their food choices. By offering an alternative to the "low-class" option of cheap, industrially produced convenience foods, these programs are comparable to the meal assembly businesses discussed in chapter 2. Such programming offers the "modern" viewer a formula for bridging traditional expectations with the realities of contemporary life by acknowledging the limitations of time and money confronting many contemporary households. These programs—including *30 Minute Meals, Quick Fix Meals with Robin Miller, Semi-Homemade Cooking with Sandra Lee, 5 Ingredient Fix, Ten Dollar Dinners with Melissa d'Arabian, Sandra's Money Saving Meals,* and *Good Deal with Dave Lieberman*—share tips and strategies for coping with these realities. In doing so, they also feature an increased focus on "health" as they typically emphasize that their time-saving and cost-saving strategies still allow home cooks to provide healthy meals for their families.

Like the meal assembly businesses that we discussed in chapter 2, these programs make subtle gestures toward class as they link time, money, and health to distinguish middle-class families who strive to maintain the sacrosanct family meal despite the pressures of modern American life from presumably working-class families who rely on fast and processed foods that may save time and money but that ultimately cost families both their health and their precious quality time. The overwhelming whiteness of these programs also signals how this class hierarchy is racialized, with white families presumably making every effort to maintain the tradition of the family meal while non-white families flock to fast food restaurants or depend on cheap, processed foods to feed their families. To follow the lead of these programs is ostensibly to make the "right" choice, which pays off in health and quality of life; it also garners status, especially when compared to those who make "bad" choices that, as the argument goes, undermine our collective well-being. At the same time, these shows—like all Food Network programs—rely on a clear separation between the middle-class environments in which they are situated and the off-camera staff whose invisible work makes them possible. While the balance between the discourses of gender, class, and health varies among these many programs, what they collectively reveal is the Food Network's ability to adapt its programming in the face of shifting social priorities and values even as it sustains its promise of access to the transformative power of culinary capital to its viewers. As Signe Rousseau notes, "the more food media we consume, the less incentive we have to think for ourselves about how we eat" (2012, xx); the more alluring and adaptable the models of selfhood offered in cookery programs, the more we viewers are enticed to "go along to get along."

Such adaptability takes its most extreme form in our third category, "competitive" programming, which includes shows that offer new frameworks for thinking about food and the kind of identities that it can promote via the circulation of culinary capital. Current Food Network shows that we place in this category include *Iron Chef America*, *Food Network Challenge*, *The Next Food Network Star*, *Chopped*, *Ultimate Recipe Showdown*, *Dinner: Impossible*, and *Throwdown with Bobby Flay*. Such programming draws upon the genre of reality television in general, and competitive programming in particular, to shift the terrain upon which culinary capital circulates.

In the competitive programming format, cooking is less about meeting one's familial or social obligations and more about confronting a challenge and persevering despite harsh conditions. Although food remains the central element of these programs, a heightened emphasis on the culinary skills and abilities of the chefs suggests that there is more at stake than one's responsibilities to one's family. Reputations are on the line as chefs strive to affirm their culinary prowess by beating challengers—not only other chefs, but also limited resources and a ticking clock. In short, it is less about demonstrating the feminine attributes assigned traditionally to the wife, mother, and hostess and more about embracing the masculine traits of strength, vigor, and authority.

Clearly, when the Food Network decided in 2001 to change its strategy and to begin using adventure and travel to target men (Ketchum 2007, 167), it also relied on familiar tropes—for instance, the overt masculinization of the kitchen as "Kitchen Stadium" on *Iron Chef America*—to make that audience feel more comfortable stepping up to the stove. Such programming suggests a more traditionally masculine aesthetic and, in doing so, shifts the terms upon which culinary capital is acquired and circulated. "By supporting hegemonic masculinity rather than a domestic masculinity, competitive contests counter constructions of cooking as nurturing, democratic and family-centered labor" (Swenson 2009, 50), and thus they largely preserve a traditional gender dichotomy. In doing so, they offer viewers a road-tested mode of masculinity based in conquest and triumph that still provides for the acquisition of culinary capital and the cachet in mainstream quarters that comes with it.

At the same time, food scholar Fabio Parasecoli notes that masculinities are not eternally fixed, but instead that "as practices, they sometimes articulate contradictory desires, emotions, and ideals, denying the notion of a static and defined identity" (2008, 98). Thus, even as these programs seem to promote a familiar and rigid form of hegemonic masculinity, they can also signal a more complex and ambivalent performance of gender. In fact, while we necessarily limit our discussion to a few specific shows within each category, we recognize that the full roster of Food Network programming offers a rather nuanced representation of gender, with some programs actually blurring gender boundaries, perhaps acknowledging a broader cultural shift in the rigidity of assigned gender roles.

For example, while programs in our "traditional" category tend to feature women who are identified primarily as wives and mothers and who are situated either within their own home kitchens or in carefully constructed facsimiles of such a traditionally feminine environment, there are other programs that feature male hosts. A show like *Tyler's Ultimate*, hosted by Tyler Florence, is scheduled during the daytime, which the network promotes as featuring more "instructional" programming most often framed as helping viewers achieve personal satisfaction in the kitchen while they fulfill familial obligations traditionally assigned to women. However, because one possible aim of such a show is to attract male viewers who are more likely to identify with Florence than with female hosts, it features several subtle elements that give it a more masculine flair, including an urban industrial set design and a premise that emphasizes Florence's expertise—a quality usually underplayed in other programs in this category—as he offers the "ultimate" version of familiar recipes.

Similarly, in our "modern" category, shows like *Good Deal with Dave Lieberman* and *Down Home with the Neelys* feature male hosts or cohosts, again signaling a desire on the part of the Food Network to broaden its viewership in ways that both rely upon and complicate familiar assumptions about gender and cooking. At the same time, *Down Home with the Neelys* signals the network's effort to broaden the racial diversity of its programming. As Patrick and Gina Neely are presented as an effusively happy black, middle-class, hetero family, they simultaneously introduce and seek to overcome racial difference. At the same time, it is interesting to note that the most visible black male on the network is incorporated into the traditional feminine space of the home kitchen (though he spends a great deal of time at the backyard barbeque so as not to completely undermine his masculinity) and is most often portrayed as docile in relation to his wife. Through such shows, male viewers are invited to undertake projects of the self that blur normative boundaries of gender, class, and race as they take on the work of becoming better cooks, better providers for their families, and more well-rounded men. As such, these shows can be read as offering an alternative mode of masculinity that confers distinction upon those men who take the risk of doing this work.

In this context, it is also important to note that historically too little attention has been paid to the ways in which ideologies of masculinity as related to food are changing (Julier and Lindenfeld 2005). While the surge in cookbooks addressed to men from the mid-1940s to 1960 reassured readers that barbecuing was appropriately masculine and that cooking was just a hobby (Neuhaus 2003), the recent explosion in male-targeted competitive cooking shows assuages a different set of anxieties about masculinity. Specifically, we are interested in how such programming provides its viewers with a means of acquiring culinary capital that reasserts rather than undermines masculinity. We read this shift against the backdrop of a broader "threat" to traditional notions of masculinity witnessed in the queering of contemporary American popular culture in general, and in the most recent iterations of reality television and lifestyle programming in particular.

But even as programs like *Queer Eye for the Straight Guy* introduced the term "metrosexual" into the American lexicon and as gay men became increasingly visible as both participants in and consumers of such programming, television also provided a means of defending masculinity from this queering of American popular culture. Perhaps unexpectedly, recent iterations of food programming, with their promise of culinary capital acquired through victory in competition, have played an important role in this process. As Rebecca Swenson contends, "cooking discourse no longer warns men that the kitchen is not their lair; yet, cooking is still negotiated in ways that protect the concept of masculinity" (2007, 21). It is also noteworthy that when women are featured in such programming—as competitive celebrity chefs, as an "Iron Chef" (in the case of Cat Cora), and as contestants and judges—they become implicated in this protection of hegemonic masculinity through the on-set performance of what gender theorist Judith Halberstam calls "female

masculinity" even as they complicate the gendered narratives that such programs circulate (Halberstam 1998).

This claim is consistent with the work of T.J.M. Holden (2005), whose study
of Japanese food television argues that it communicates a particularly hegemonic masculinity, characterized by authority, power, and possession, and that
these traits are exhibited not only by men, but also by women who adopt and
reinforce them. Men may be the most obvious parties to gain status from their
food-related performances of competitive masculinity, particularly in working-
class milieus or environments saturated by traditional and rigid concepts of
appropriate gender role behavior. But in other fields, especially those marked
by higher socioeconomic status where more progressive perspectives on gender
flexibility and the desirability of androgyny prevail, women too gain status by
flexing their culinary muscles.

SITUATING THE FOOD NETWORK

While the Food Network has contributed to a dramatic expansion in the breadth
and range of food-related programming, the role of such programming in representing and shaping attitudes about gender and class can be traced back
to its origins. Dating back to the earliest days of television, cooking shows
fell initially under the rubric of educational programming, featuring either male
hosts like James Beard or Graham Kerr, whose culinary knowledge, skills, and
expertise classified them as gourmets—galloping or otherwise—or female
hosts like Julia Child who downplayed formal training and expertise as she
created a persona that propelled her to the top of this genre. These programs
were pitched primarily to female viewers as a vital resource for helping them
fulfill their socially prescribed roles as wives and mothers, a goal that would
bring with it the promise of status: the "good wife," the "good mother." At the
same time, they invited these women to develop their culinary skills while exercising their creativity and validating their social position. In this regard, they
are connected very closely to the meal assembly kitchens and their historical antecedents that we discussed in chapter 2. Since those early days, food
television has morphed from not terribly flashy how-to cooking shows "hosted
by prim home economists and righteous nutritionists" to recipe instruction
shows with studio audiences and charismatic hosts to the present configuration, involving celebrity chefs, the competitive element of much reality television, and elements of contemporary travel programming (K. Collins 2008). In
charting this evolution in food programming, Kathleen Collins suggests that
one of the "advantageous conditions" that has contributed to its continued
popularity and success has been a gradual shift from "the inhospitable mindset of the Early Period—food is sustenance and cooking is a chore" toward

an "interest in food as cultural capital and a form of self-expression" (2008). Collins contends that cooking shows are a "unique social barometer" whose legacy "corresponds to the transitioning of women at home to women at work, from eight- to twenty-four-hour workdays, from cooking as domestic labor to enjoyable leisure, and from clearly defined to more fluid gender roles" (K. Collins 2009, 5). As the shows have shifted from being instructional to being entertaining, they are now less about how to cook and more about how to live; as such, they participate in the process of producing proper citizens that results in the accretion of culinary capital. While Collins identifies this cultural shift in attitudes toward food as contributing to the continued success of televised food programming, we are interested in the role that such programming plays in generating and negotiating such attitudinal changes. In other words, we explore how such programming produces and circulates the culinary capital upon which it depends for its continued success.

One way that it does so is by utilizing explicitly or implicitly the discourse of self-improvement. By watching such programming, acquiring the knowledge and skills that it imparts, and using this newly acquired culinary capital in their lives, viewers can affirm their social position and strengthen their sense of self. Of course, there is an important distinction to be made between how such programming is marketed, or what implicit promises it contains—in our analysis, culinary capital for the viewer via his or her acquisition of skills and knowledge—and how viewers *use* such programming—which appears to be more in the vein of self-making than practical know-how (Bower 2004). Food programming, with its promise of personal transformation, functions as a means of circulating culinary capital and inviting both participants and viewers to use this newly acquired capital to effect change in their lives. In doing so, individuals make choices and aspire to lifestyle practices that reflect not only specific culinary trends, but also the prevailing ideologies that inform them; as Rousseau notes, food media encourage identification with certain priorities through an active process of distraction from political, economic, and social responsibilities (2012). While this particular type of programming has historically been aimed at women—as it provided them a means of embracing their culinary responsibilities and using them to bolster their own sense of identity as they transform the domestic sphere (Ketchum 2005)—in recent years, this particular formula, while still evident, has also begun to share air time with food-related programming that circulates culinary capital in a number of other ways while promoting a range of social identities.

Across the typology of shows that frame our discussion is one commonplace: the celebrity chef, who audiences not only want to cook like, but to *live* like. Television scholar Megan Mullen notes that Food Network stars balance culinary credentials with charisma to draw an audience. "Moreover, the programs manage to flatter any degree of culinary savvy their viewers might possess, while subtly poking fun at the elitism that traditionally has lent legitimacy to that type of knowledge. Food Network's programs also cue its audiences to certain types of viewing sensibilities and by extension to types of cultural connoisseurship" (Mullen 2008, 119; see also Bell 2002). According to Mullen, the Food Network actively targets not only affluent consumers but those lower in economic and cultural capital, for obvious reasons—the greater potential for profit. Part of the profit comes from selling luxury versions of everyday goods (food, kitchen gear, etc.) to people who might not otherwise be able to afford luxury on big ticket items, and from selling special, authentic experiences to busy, affluent consumers who care more about experiences than about products or goods (Mullen 2008, 120). Our analysis of Food Network programs exposes the range of strategies of identification employed in food television programming that promotes consumer pleasure and corporate profit. Our findings make us, along with food and media studies scholar Laura Lindenfeld, wary of expecting a great deal of transformative potential from this newly nichified mass medium (Lindenfeld 2010). We conclude that while such programs entice viewers with overt and covert promises of self-transformation, what ultimately transforms is the network's programming as it adapts to changes in society, in general, and the broader television landscape, in particular, a trend noted by Laurie Ouellette and James Hay (2008).

This emphasis on self-realization and self-transformation as the promise of televised food programming marks a change in its marketing as it adapts to important shifts in the gender and class ideologies that have informed such programming from its inception. Ashley, Hollows, Jones, and Taylor (2004) focus specifically on this change when they argue that in the new television configuration, cooking becomes less about caring for others and more about caring for the self. "If the care performed by the new television chefs is based around a self that finds food a source of pleasure and entertainment, then this also works to suggest that the care invested in the meal is not a product of domestic labour but 'aestheticized leisure'" (Ashley et al. 2004, 183). It is this intricate transition from "domestic labour" to "aestheticized leisure" that signals the inevitable, though often invisible, links between gender and class that inform our analysis.

In short, we argue that from their inception to their most current variations, televised cooking shows are intimately connected with the creation and circulation of culinary capital as a crucial vehicle for ideologies of gender and class. Referring to Emeril Lagasse, Toby Miller (2007) writes that "crass working-class credentialism has displaced Child-ish blue-blood shamateur excellence. A popularization is underway far beyond the cryptocommodified, quasi-bake-sale-funded, kindness-of-strangers-like-you ghetto of PBS. The Food Network has constructed sophisticated links to retail chains and the Internet, and transcended gender and class divisions in the audience by making gourmet food available beyond the sphere of conventional cultural capital" (Miller 2007, 132). Miller's commentary is worth dissecting for the way in which it fuses a critique of gender-inflected class politics. Julia Child, the blue-blood woman, has been replaced by not just Emeril, but a bunch of working- and lower-middle-class white guys. Guy Fieri, host of *Diners, Drive-ins, and Dives*, as well as celebrity chefs Tom Colicchio, Charlie Palmer, Michael Romano, and Todd English, who all aspired to "move on up" in society, were people for whom "the life of the kitchen afforded . . . a new kind of upward mobility, a career path and identity at once connected with their roots and offering expansive possibilities" (Hyman 2008, 44). They ride the crest of the integrated global marketing platforms of network television; in short, they are propelled by capital and its democratic promises to the "everyman."

In much the same way that Megan Mullen notes that the Food Network "manages to strike a balance between elite tastes and popular culture, between snobbism and populism, between cooking and eating, and between work and leisure" (2008, 115), it also slyly proposes a fairly broad repertoire of gender and class performances, offering a little something for everyone. At the same time, while the programming on the Food Network continues to feature predominantly white chefs, judges, contestants, and cuisines, the Cooking Channel makes a more consistent nod to cultural and culinary otherness. Shows like *Caribbean Food Made Easy, Chinese Food Made Easy, Indian Food Made Easy, Everyday Exotic, Luke Nguyen's Vietnam, Simply Delicioso with Ingrid Hoffmann, Spice Goddess*, and *Viva Daisy!* demonstrate the network's recognition of racial and ethnic difference as an important component of its audience appeal. Simultaneously, such programs emphasize cultural and culinary differences while promising to teach viewers how to overcome them. Ultimately, both the Food Network and the Cooking Channel aim to produce ideal "consumer citizens" who aspire to reproduce the lifestyles they witness on television and, by doing so, to acquire their share of status through consumerism. Whether viewers are content simply to follow suit is an important question, but it is a first step to note that what the Food Network promises will bring distinction is actually rather limited. Such programming links individual patterns of consumption to the broader project of subject formation as it seeks to produce self-governing citizens who have internalized a broad range of prevailing values and ideologies.

This may very well be just the point about culinary capital and the Food Network: as the culture industries busily feed consumers fantasies infused with a range of gender and class performances that allow them to feel "in the know" and to claim enhanced status, those same consumers do not necessarily stop to think about what may be missing from the screen, and more importantly, from their lives. Signe Hansen argues that "that the real product of food media is not the celebrity chef, but the consumer. Food media creates a base of consumers whose appetites are literally and figuratively kept wanting; this is the new business of food" (2008, 49). As Cheri Ketchum contends, the Food Network's strategy of "encouraging viewers to obtain and use a wide range of consumer goods and promoting restaurant experiences to confer symbolic status on individuals" has very successfully served the interests of the network, its sponsors, and of consumers (2007, 171)—but what about the interests of citizens?

Undeniably, the lifestyles promised on the Food Network function as an appealing consumer carrot even as the network turns steep profits for food- and lifestyle-industry mavens, but perhaps we should not so readily ignore the stick: the slick consumer approach obscures any serious address of the audience as citizens insofar as food is concerned (Ketchum 2005; Miller 2007; Retzinger 2008). The upshot of food television's popularity is the sym- bolic democratization of culinary capital—viewers are authorized to sit around feeling entitled and in-the-know, without really thinking about what is miss- ing from their basis of knowledge. While we are not suggesting that viewers are inevitably passive dupes to the all-powerful media, we do recognize that sometimes the deck can be stacked in ways that constrain the possibilities for resistance.

Because it harnesses the integrated platforms of global media, lifestyle programming, in general, and food television, in particular, are adept at cur- tailing resistance by giving everyday citizens less room to talk back, to read against the grain, and so on. As we noted in an earlier work, while "food and food practices may be read as disrupting class hierarchies as they provide their consumers with access to a world normally out of reach from their eco- nomic position...because such access is limited and temporary, it ultimately does not challenge dominant ideologies of class. To the contrary, it protects them by providing consumers with an illusion of access that contradicts the reality of their economic and social positions" (LeBesco and Naccarato 2008, 224). Kathleen Collins likewise notes that viewability does not equal accessi- bility, and that "for a large element of society, time and money are obstacles to the cultural trading up that beckons us" (2009, 225).

Given the current climate of pro-media business deregulatory policies, where "the dominant interpellation is about learning to govern the self through orderly preparation, style, and pleasure—the transformation of po- tential drudgery into a special event, and the incorporation of difference into a treat rather than a threat" (Miller 2007, 143), we might be well advised to avoid over-investing in television as a key site for the transformation that would make the politics of food central to quotidian citizenship. As we trace the evolution of the Food Network's programming, we are interested in how it reacts to a shifting cultural landscape by producing shows that run the gamut from maintaining a lineage with traditional cooking shows to adapting such programs in the face of modern stresses on individuals and families, to creating entirely new platforms that incorporate a variety of gimmicks popularized across the reality television genre. While the network's programming continuously undergoes its own transformations, one thing remains constant: in each of its manifestations, it makes a false promise to its audience that culinary capital is the result and catalyst of personal transformation when, in fact, it functions much more as a means of sustaining the gender and class ideologies that make extremely unlikely the radical social transformation that might obliterate or seriously disrupt our need to stratify and assert distinction. To illustrate this point, we examine three genres of Food Network programming in the sections that follow, paying particular attention to the ways each links gender, class, and culinary capital.

TRADITIONAL PROGRAMMING

Perhaps one of the Food Network's most successful personalities, Paula Deen hosts several shows, including *Paula's Home Cooking*, *Paula's Best Dishes*, and *Paula's Party*. It is in Deen's personal biography that we find one of the few overt references to economic class across this type of programming. In fact, Deen's biography on the Food Network website touts her rags-to-riches story presumably because it epitomizes the notion that culinary capital can transform lives. Identifying Deen as a "self-made success story who learned the secrets of Southern cooking from her Grandmother some 30 years ago," this biography goes on to explain that as a divorced mother of two young children, with only $200 in her pocket, she moved with her sons to Savannah, where she started her own catering company. "Most days Paula rose in the early morning to grill chicken for her popular chicken salad. Every Thursday night she cooked until the wee hours to create a mouthwatering Friday barbecue special, Boston Butt. Her local specialties, such as chicken pot pies, barbecue sandwiches, lasagna and banana pudding, caught on with the Savannah business crowd and quickly became the talk of the town." Eventually, Deen opened her own restaurant, The Lady and Sons, first in the Savannah Best Western and later in a more preferable downtown location. Her success as a restaurateur and as a Food Network personality has also led to other successes; she has published several cookbooks and currently publishes her own magazine, *Cooking with Paula Deen*.

Despite this significant success as a restaurateur and businesswoman, Deen's Food Network programs, most notably *Paula's Home Cooking*, situate her less in this context and more in that of mother, home cook, and caretaker. In fact, her two sons, Bobby and Jamie, are regular guests and have developed their own show on the Food Network, *Road Tasted*. To further establish

Deen's identity as a "family woman," the Food Network invited her fans to share in her recent marriage, and her husband, Michael, has become an integral part of her show through both his appearances in specific episodes and the many references Deen makes to him as she fulfills her role as traditional wife who satisfies his culinary needs by preparing his favorite dishes.

In addition to this familiar identification as wife and mother, Deen is also framed by her Southern roots, which serve to balance her rags-to-riches biography so as to maintain her working-class credentials even as she attains greater economic success. This balancing act is achieved, first and foremost, by her cuisine. In describing *Paula's Home Cooking*, the Food Network website emphasizes Deen's "small-town life" and her focus on "uncomplicated and delicious home cooking." Stories of family and friends blend with the culinary knowledge and skills that she acquired at her grandmother's side to recreate the classic "country kitchen." The Food Network's list of Deen's top 100 recipes supports these characterizations; the list includes such Southern staples as chicken and rice casserole, Lady and Sons chicken pot pie, chicken and dumplings, Southern fried chicken, gumbo, chili, old-fashioned meatloaf, macaroni and cheese, and Cajun shrimp. Highlighted dessert recipes include bananas foster, slow berry cobbler, the Lady and Sons peach cobbler, key lime pie, lemon meringue pie, chocolate mousse pie, low country cookies, and s'more brulee, to mention only a few of the over 400 dessert recipes Deen has contributed to the website. The unmistakable regional identification of these dishes both relies upon and promotes certain class-based assumptions; namely, that her Southern tastes resist "high-class" presumptions and refuse modification based on the contemporary trend toward "healthy" eating. Deen is, first and foremost, a Southern cook who uses her culinary knowledge and skills to honor her heritage and celebrate and support her family. While Deen can be said to culinarily capitalize on conventional ideologies of gender, she resists trading on notions of elite class status in favor of down-home regional parochialism—a sleight of hand made all the more intriguing by her material success as a national television personality and entrepreneur.

At the same time that Deen's cooking honors her heritage, there are questions about whose heritage is elided in her work. Some contend that Southern food is essentially the same thing as soul food, and that region is a more important determinant than race, as poor and working-class whites and blacks in the South traditionally eat more like one another than they do like Northerners or people who are more economically well-off (Opie 2008, 130; Witt 2004, 97). But it is also possible to read Deen as a throwback to the pre-1960s white Southerners who published cookbooks filled with "Southern" dishes that Black Arts leaders like Amiri Baraka claimed originated in the black belt of the South, founded by African Americans (Opie 2008, 133);

understandably, this kind of appropriation rankles, especially when it redirects fame and fortune away from African Americans.

Concerns over the economics of Deen's cuisine abound. Historically, the ethos of soul food involved making do with what one had and finding tasty uses for the parts of animals cast off by masters to slaves; bottom line, it was inexpensive and demonstrated ingenuity and creativity. That very quality of soul food—its ability to signify survival and empowerment—led to its appropriation as "the revolutionary high cuisine of bourgeoisie African Americans" (Opie 2008, 132) in the 1960s during the civil rights and Black Power movements. But as Doris Witt notes, "the discourse of soul was problematic not simply because white people were appropriating it and not simply because it was associated with the much maligned black middle class," who were considered race traitors, trading on the Otherness of their poor brethren in order to solidify an authentic identity for themselves; "the discourse was problematic because it also encoded American culture's ambivalent attitude toward black women, its desire for black female nurture and its concomitant fear of black female control" (Witt 2004, 183). Thus, Deen's embrace of Southern cooking and soul food in her performance of culinary capital is necessarily inflected by racial and gendered class politics.

While at first glance there seem to be few similarities between Paula Deen and Food Network darling Giada De Laurentiis, a comparison between them and their programs reveals how the Food Network employs different strategies to serve a common purpose. De Laurentiis's Food Network biography, like Deen's, situates the roots of her culinary interests and training with her family. Whereas Deen learned at the side of her Southern grandmother, De Laurentiis "grew up in a large Italian family where the culture of food was a staple in and of itself" and "consistently found herself in the family's kitchen and spent a great deal of time at her grandfather's restaurant, DDL Foodshow." Thus, her "passion for food" was well nurtured even as she studied anthropology at the University of California, Los Angeles. She ultimately decided to pursue a culinary career, beginning with her training at Le Cordon Bleu in Paris and continuing with positions at the Ritz Carlton Fine Dining Room and Wolfgang Puck's Spago in Beverly Hills. She eventually started her own catering company, GDL Foods. Thus, by the time she joined the Food Network in 2002, De Laurentiis had acquired impressive culinary training and gained significant professional experience. However, while she brought these credentials to the Food Network (and they are highlighted in her biography), they are not a central element of the persona she projects on her television shows, including *Everyday Italian* and *Giada at Home*.

Like *Paula's Home Cooking*, both *Everyday Italian* and *Giada at Home* place De Laurentiis in a domestic rather than professional kitchen, and most episodes include a narrative set-up that emphasizes caretaking and nurturing.

In *Everyday Italian*, De Laurentiis most frequently cooks for friends and family, with episodes ending with her and her usually hip and attractive friends enjoying the fruits of her labor. While this format replicates to some extent that of *Paula's Home Cooking* as it evokes the pleasure of cooking for family and friends, it does so in a way that emphasizes a certain youthful contemporariness and signals an important generational shift. This is evidenced by the Food Network's description of her cuisine, explaining that she "shares updated versions of the homey recipes she grew up with in her Italian family." While her emphasis on transforming classic Italian recipes to make them quicker and healthier signals a shift toward the more "modern" types of shows we discuss next, these attributes are certainly not central to the identity of either *Everyday Italian* or *Giada at Home*; at the same time, there are other ways in which these shows reinforce the kinds of traditional class and gender ideologies that link them more strongly with *Paula's Home Cooking*. As both shows situate De Laurentiis in a more contemporary, though nonetheless domestic, context, they also suggest a level of economic and culinary capitalization attained by both De Laurentiis and her friends. Episodes in the later seasons of *Everyday Italian* are marked by a gradual transition in De Laurentiis's television persona as they featured increasing references to her courtship, marriage, and new motherhood; this shift culminated in her new show, *Giada at Home*, which adds luster to De Laurentiis's sheen of traditional femininity. While presenting a more modern version of femininity than that offered by Deen, De Laurentiis similarly downplays her own expertise and lifestyle-maven ambitions, as well as her elite class status, capitalizing instead on an accessible, updated "girl next door" persona that has recently evolved into a contemporary version of the traditional wife and mother.

Ultimately, both programs invite viewers to share in a set of culinary rituals and practices that serve to sustain traditional gender and class ideologies. Insofar as Paula Deen's rags-to-riches story suggests that cooking fueled her meteoric rise to successful restaurateur and Food Network celebrity, it promotes a version of class mobility that obscures how the Food Network in general, and Deen's celebrity chef status in particular, support the very capitalist machinery that makes such economic mobility very unlikely (LeBesco and Naccarato 2008). Deen embraces her television persona as the traditional wife who labors selflessly in the kitchen to feed her loving husband and children. She promotes such an identification to her fans, supports the gender ideologies that inform it, and masks her own ability to transcend this persona as she has achieved remarkable success as an entrepreneur and businesswoman. Even as she has done so, however, she continues to use her television programs, and their depiction of her food choices and practices, to maintain a down-home, Southern identity that gives her a unique form of authenticity that the Food Network markets to its viewers.

In the case of De Laurentiis, while her programs, her cuisine, and her persona are modernized, they nonetheless function to promote familiar gender and class ideologies. By crafting a television persona that masks her culinary training, these shows reinforce familiar narratives in which women learn to cook from their families and grow naturally into their domestic roles in their households. As her persona has shifted from that of a hip, young, single woman who entertains her friends to a loving wife and mother who embraces her traditional role within her family, the message to her fans remains the same; namely, that her identity—and theirs to the extent that they aspire to mimic her idealized lifestyle—is grounded firmly in the kitchen. Like in the case of Deen, De Laurentiis's persona as traditional, if updated, wife and mother is one that necessarily obscures her professional success not only as a television personality, but as a savvy marketer of her cookbooks and line of cookware. At the same time, while markers of class status can be read in the perfectly appointed kitchens and other settings for her programs, any specific references to class are muted as De Laurentiis's culinary practices and the broader lifestyle around which they are framed rely upon an "everywoman" persona that make them marketable to the widest possible audience. The implicit promise is clear: whichever chef a viewer chooses to emulate, using homemade food to nurture and care for friends and family marks that viewer in positive ways, rewarding him/her with status for his/her efforts and talents. In short, as they offer viewers their own share of the culinary capital displayed by Deen and De Laurentiis, these programs rehearse familiar tropes to reinforce traditional ideologies of gender and class. In doing so, they demonstrate how culinary capital shapes the social spaces within which individual identities are constructed and maintained.

We might stop to wonder why these prominent representations of traditional feminine domesticity are so popular *now*, at a time when we imagine ourselves more liberated than ever before. Perhaps it is because feminists and women at home have "gotten out" to do wage work in record numbers that these images are being offered to us (Ray 2007, 52), in much the same way that *Leave It to Beaver*–style 1950s televisual imaginings functioned as soothing, nostalgic hedges against the reality of women's newfound power (Spigel 1992). Like the marketing of the meal assembly kitchens and e-grocers that we discussed in chapter 2, these programs allow viewers to imagine themselves maintaining the traditional models of femininity and family that they promote while masking the extent to which they reinforce the very gender ideologies through which the pressure to conform to these "ideals" are sustained. Nonetheless, these traditional images are far from the only game in town as the Food Network offers a little something for everyone in terms of gender and class ideologies, all the better to reach disparate segments of its niche audience.

MODERN PROGRAMMING

Following the tremendous success of Rachael Ray's *30 Minute Meals*, as evidenced not only by the show's popularity but also by the countless products and cookbooks that it spawned, the Food Network moved quickly to emulate what proved to be a very successful format. With a nod to the modern woman who wants to fulfill her traditional role as homemaker while struggling to do so in the face of time constraints, *Quick Fix Meals with Robin Miller* is described on the Food Network website as recognizing the reality of modern life: "Busy people everywhere face the same dilemma—how to get healthy weeknight dinners on the table with only minutes to spare." It also claims to provide solutions to this vexing problem: "Robin Miller guides us through the landmines of getting food on the table nightly with her stress-free meal-planning strategies." She does so by offering "easy, day-to-day plans" aimed at "help[ing] even the novice cook master these quick and tasty recipes." Emphasizing time management, Miller's recipes begin by listing the "weekend prep" that can be done in advance and include complete shopping lists, so that "you only have to hit the store once." With many recipes, she emphasizes how they can yield multiple servings throughout the week and in other episodes she offers time-saving hints like using one main ingredient to create several different dishes.

Like other network personalities, Miller has translated her program's format into a series of successful cookbooks whose titles emphasize a speedy and heroic home cook, including *Quick Fix Meals*, *Robin to the Rescue*, and *Robin Rescues Dinner*. However, these books underscore the balance she seeks to strike between the quality of her recipes as judged in terms of both taste and healthiness and the efficiency of her process. *Quick Fix Meals*, for example, emphasizes "time-saving strategies" and organizes recipes around some of Miller's patented techniques: Meal Kits, Morph-It Recipes, Greased Lightning (super fast recipes), Simple Sides, and In-a-Snap Sweets. These options are particularly appealing to women, whose participation in what sociologist Arlie Russell Hochshild (1989) has called "the second shift" means that large numbers of them are working outside the home but that expectations about their provision of domestic labor, which includes cooking for the family, are not at all diminished after they come home (see also Inness 2001). From its title to its audience pitch, Miller's show focuses on time, challenging the assumption that one must sacrifice preparing quality food if one is to keep up with the demands of an increasingly fast-paced society. If the traditional cooking shows discussed above seem only minimally impacted, if at all, by the quickening pace of modern society, this reality provides the underlying premise for Miller's show and its success suggests that it has connected with a significant number of viewers. By acknowledging that the viewer is pressed for time, Miller strikes a chord with viewers who recognize that the hard work of spending all day cooking for family and friends requires a lot more leisure time than they have.[2] She reassures them that they will still be seen as good providers if they at least make an effort to go "homemade," however much a Deen or a De Laurentiis may regard the integrity of that "homemade" as compromised. At the same time, Miller's series falls short of a feminist, worker-centered manifesto in that it fails to urge its audience to question the very system that demands women's harried acquiescence and instead, like the marketing of the meal assembly kitchens and e-grocers we discussed in chapter 2, encourages them to embrace the mantra of the Superwoman.

While Miller's approach emphasizes time-saving techniques and strategies, another popular show pushes even further in this direction. According to the network's website, *Semi-Homemade with Sandra Lee*, which premiered in 2003, had "one of the highest-rated daytime launches in the network's history and still remains a consistent top-performing daytime program." The site credits host Sandra Lee with developing her "semi-homemade" philosophy out of necessity: "The oldest of five children, Sandra helped her mother manage the household and the kids while the family lived on food stamps and welfare. She quickly learned how to turn budget-friendly products into delicious and special meals for the family." If Miller's raison d'être is helping women meet the obligations of their traditional gender roles in the face of modern limitations upon their time, then Lee's narrative relies upon a much more overt link between gender and class as she connects gender ideology—it was her mother who was responsible for managing the household and the children—with the harsh reality of poverty as the dual motivations for her culinary philosophy and eventual success. Just as with Deen's personal story, the acquisition of culinary capital is at the heart of Lee's rags-to-riches story. Her biography on the Food Network website explains that from her humble roots, Lee emerged as "an internationally-acclaimed home and style expert" whose "70/30 Semi-Homemade philosophy combines 70 percent ready-made products with 30 percent fresh and creative touches and allows everyone the time and confidence to create something that looks, feels or tastes from scratch." Having studied at Le Cordon Bleu, she came to believe that "her Semi-Homemade philosophy and savvy shortcuts could be applied toward gourmet recipes so that every over-extended homemaker could create and savor delicious dishes at home in less time and at a fraction of the cost." Like Robin Miller, Lee is less concerned with challenging a gender and class ideology that expects an "over-extended [presumably female] homemaker" to continue bearing primary responsibility for preparing her family's meals and focuses, instead, she is focused on providing such women with a grab bag of gimmicks and shortcuts for accomplishing this task given limitations of time and money.

Like 1950s housewives who were invited to take advantage of new kitchen technologies in their efforts to meet their domestic responsibilities (Holliday 2001), viewers of *Semi-Homemade Cooking* are encouraged to use modern conveniences to create meals that are less time-consuming but that are still nutritious and delicious. While Lee's approach has invited sharp criticism from tradition-minded cooks or formally trained chefs who see such shortcuts as compromising the quality of the finished product, such controversies ultimately expose a familiar class-based elitism. Those who carp that canned stock is not the same as homemade, premade pie crusts are not the same as those made from scratch, Cool Whip is not freshly whipped cream, and boxed, canned, or frozen products are not the same as fresh ingredients presumably have—or want to appear to have—the luxury of dismissing the realities of time and money faced by those who do the home cooking these days. Such condemnation has both gendered and class-based overtones insofar as it contrasts elite, professional, high-end cuisine typically associated with men with the unpaid domestic cooking traditionally and still primarily associated with women that is downgraded even further when it relies on quick or inexpensive substitutes for time-laden and/or costly recipes and techniques. While fans celebrate Lee's approach, critics refuse to grant Lee's efforts the status of "cooking," suggesting that even as the Food Network adapts its programming to appeal to contemporary women who are confronting limited time and money with which to fulfill their familial obligations, they need to maintain traditional programs so as not to alienate viewers with more traditional expectations of appropriate gender role behavior, of quality food, and of the relationship between the two. Such debates exemplify the value of culinary capital and reveal what is at stake as the means through which it is circulated are reimagined.[3] In addition, they provide an opening for the emergence of a new form of gendered culinary capital that challenges the assumption that the kitchen is the space for performances of only feminine domestic labor.

Such a transition is furthered by programs that shift the focus more fully from constraints of time to constraints of money. The winner of season five of *The Next Food Network Star*, Melissa d'Arabian, now hosts *Ten Dollar Dinners with Melissa d'Arabian*, which is described on the Food Network website as "show[ing] viewers how to incorporate creative and tasty meals into their budgets by sharing her tried-and-true recipes. With countless tips to save time and money in the kitchen, she keeps her $10 promise in every episode: four people, ten bucks, infinite possibilities."

Similarly, Sandra Lee's new program, *Sandra's Money Saving Meals*, adapts her 70/30 philosophy to emphasize its cost-saving benefits in addition to its time-saving advantages. The website describes the show as "featur[ing] incredible budget-friendly recipes for every day of the week." It goes on to explain Lee's central goal as "maximiz[ing] cost-saving success" by "sharing unique ideas for savvy supermarket shopping and proper pantry stocking while highlighting each meal's unbeatable total price point."

While these shows mark an important shift in emphasis from gender-based to class-based identifications between host and viewer, a third program takes this transition a step further. *Good Deal with Dave Lieberman* has a similar focus on affordability while its male host complicates the gendered assumptions that may be more muted but that remain unchallenged in the "budget-conscious" programs hosted by d'Arabian and Lee. While the website's rhetoric about the show aligns it with these other programs as it promises to "giv[e] viewers practical tips on keeping quality up and costs down," it simultaneously distances itself from shows hosted by women that frame such cost-saving measures around the needs of the family. Instead, the description of Lieberman's show emphasizes entertaining, whether "preparing a buffet dinner for an ever-expanding party guest list" or "throwing an indoor BBQ party for the space/budget-challenged." All three shows imagine viewers rewarded with status for their cost-saving strategies as cooks. It is not difficult to imagine that such status and savings might then facilitate the upward social mobility that would preclude the necessity for continued attention to cost.

While all three of these shows make explicit the class-based constraints that confront the modern cook, Lieberman's show, in particular, does this while also calling into question the gendered assumptions that go unchallenged in the other programs that we have discussed. Specifically, it opens up a space for questioning the gender ideologies that inform cooking, in general, and televised cooking shows, in particular, as it raises the possibility of legitimizing masculine forms of cooking beyond the all-too-familiar trope of the man at the barbeque, which itself is complicated by Lieberman's show as it moves the barbeque from the masculine space of the outdoors to the feminized space of the kitchen. Lieberman's show, like others that frame male hosts in traditionally feminine settings, including *Down Home with the Neelys*, *Easy Entertaining with Michael Chiarello*, *Jamie at Home*, *Tyler's Ultimate*, and *What Would Brian Boitano Make?*, signal the extent to which the Food Network has shifted the gendered terrain of its programming in order to market status through cooking to male viewers without it being configured as a threat to their masculinity. In doing so, they open the door for a more nuanced exercise of gender in televised food programming, a door which our next category kicks wide open.

COMPETITIVE PROGRAMMING

Two shows, *Dinner: Impossible* and *Throwdown with Bobby Flay*, provide insight into how this shift toward competitive food programming signals a simultaneous transition in the gender ideology that informs and is promoted by it. *Dinner: Impossible* makes overt gestures to both gender and class by referencing in its title and framing devices *Mission: Impossible*, the popular late-1960s American television show that inspired three recent Tom Cruise flicks. Each episode is framed with host chef Robert Irvine receiving the "top secret" details of his mission, delivered by a woman with a British accent via the audio system of a black, stylish BMW—sexy woman and sexy car, the ultimate conflation of gender and class in the hetero male imaginary. As Irvine accepts his mission and speeds away in the car, dramatic music and fire graphics accentuate this dramatic moment—this is masculinity writ large. *Dinner: Impossible* relies upon the dual components of surprise and limited time to create suspense. With insufficient budgets, inferior conditions, high-pressure clients, and limited ingredients, Irvine competes against himself and his circumstances as he chooses to accept each mission. From feeding 200 employees at the Mall of America, to cooking on Alcatraz, preparing an "Elvis-inspired" dinner for Priscilla Presley and 100 fans, creating a gourmet meal in the cafeteria of a high school, and catering a high-end meal for VIPs at a sporting event, using only equipment and ingredients that he acquires from tailgaters in the parking lot, *Dinner: Impossible* attempts to balance the quality of the food Irvine produces with the challenging conditions under which he produces it. In doing so, it also negotiates its dual identity: part cooking show, though very little useful culinary knowledge is imparted to viewers, and part reality competition that hinges upon whether or not Irvine can rise to the occasion and, in doing so, reassert his culinary skills as well as his cunning and grace under pressure. To succeed at this endeavor is to not simply to win a food contest, but importantly, to create a better self, a self that stands to be rewarded with status and adulation that create social and economic power.

The hyper-masculinity that saturates this show is embodied in the persona of Robert Irvine himself, from his muscular physique and overpowering personality to a biography that begins with his military service in the British Royal Navy and touts his culinary prowess; his professional resume includes cooking for the British royal family and at the White House and traveling across Europe, the Far East, the Caribbean, and the Americas. Additionally, his biography on the Food Network website is accompanied by a photo in which he wears a crisp, white, high-collared uniform, complete with a colorful emblem and monogram that blurs the line between a soldier's and a chef's formal dress. In short, there is not a hint of femininity in Irvine's persona or in the show that he hosts; rather, its format reveals its underlying function, namely, to assert Irvine's masculinity, to prove that cooking is not just for girls, and in doing so to broaden the Food Network's potential audience. The series reassures its more macho-anxious viewers that even they will be lionized for their dalliances in the kitchen—rewarded with the culinary capital that will ensure their continued success.

While the same can be said for Bobby Flay, one of America's Iron Chefs and host of several Food Network shows, including *Throwdown with Bobby Flay*, this program, in particular, offers a more restrained masculinity as Flay and his two female sidekicks engage in lighthearted competition with a variety of professional chefs and local cooking celebrities. While Flay's masculine persona has been well established through several programs, including *Boy Meets Grill*, in which he demonstrates his prowess in the traditionally male terrain of outdoor grilling, it has continued to be nurtured through his transition into more competitive-style programming, most notably *Iron Chef America.* In *Throwdown*, Flay challenges presumed experts in various types of cuisine to unexpected cook-offs. As the website's description of the show suggests, since the experts are "in their element" and Flay is "out of his," viewers can expect an "exciting, tension-filled competition." All episodes utilize the same set-up: expert chefs or local cooks are led to believe that the Food Network is taping a profile of them only to have Flay arrive and challenge them to a "throwdown," in which both Flay and guest chefs prepare their versions of the experts' signature dishes; at the end of each show, the two dishes are evaluated by judges and sampled by local participants, and a winner is declared. While these throwdowns generate a light-hearted atmosphere of friendly competition—in some instances, one chef steals ingredients from the other or spies on his competitor's activities—both chefs take these competitions seriously. Nonetheless, the convivial atmosphere often evokes more celebration than competition and Flay's ego seems well intact even when he loses to his opponents. At the same time, this show, like *Dinner: Impossible*, offers male viewers access to a form of culinary capital that nurtures, rather than challenges, their masculinity.

Several other programs, including *The Next Food Network Star*, *Ultimate Recipe Showdown*, and *Chopped*, mimic a style of competitive programming that has succeeded on other networks. Specifically, these programs incorporate elements from shows like *Survivor*, *American Idol*, *The Apprentice*, *Project Runway*, *America's Next Top Model*, and *Top Chef*, in which individuals or teams compete against each other as competitors are gradually eliminated until one person remains as the victor. To achieve the goal of culinary celebrity, both male and female challengers must augment a stereotypically feminine interest in cooking with a masculine taste for competition. In attempting to balance a coded-as-masculine egotism that is essential for creating compelling competition with a coded-as-feminine altruism that promotes identification between contestants and viewers, these series tend to utilize a common technique as they tell the stories of individual competitors as a means of evoking empathy from their audiences. In his analysis of the makeover genre, Guy Redden argues that such programs achieve a broad inclusiveness by promoting audience identification with participants through their utilization of an "intense biographical focus" (2007, 156). Such a tactic in competitive programming utilizes the personal biographies of its participants to ensure that the audience becomes invested in their stories, suffers their failures, and celebrates their successes. In doing so, the audience comes to understand and champion the transformative power of culinary capital, recognizing it as what Redden labels "a secular form of salvation" (2007, 152). It is important to note that this tactic promotes a feminine mode of identification and, in some cases, empathy between contestants and viewers while simultaneously heightening the competitive spirit of the shows. It thus puts an arguably more androgynous or gender-ambivalent spin on the requirements for possessing culinary capital.

This framework is evident in *Chopped*, in which four aspiring chefs compete against each other as they are required to combine specific wildly incompatible ingredients to prepare an appetizer, main course, and dessert that are judged by a panel of experts. After each course, one contestant is "chopped" until only one remains to claim the title of "Chopped Champion" along with a $10,000 grand prize. While on one level this show follows a familiar format that frames cooking around the competitive performance of masculinity, it also includes several features that produce a more nuanced picture as it complicates narratives of gender and class. First, host Ted Allen, who was propelled to reality show fame as food and wine expert on *Queer Eye for the Straight Guy*, complicates the show's gender dynamics. If Robert Irvine's hyper-masculinity plays an important part in gendering *Dinner: Impossible*, Allen's identification with *Queer Eye*, coupled with a less rigid performance of masculinity, creates a decidedly different tone for this program. If Irvine is muscles and machismo, Allen is slender and effeminate, broadening and diversifying the Food Network's representations of masculinity and suggesting another demographic to which it markets itself given the increased visibility of gays and lesbians as both producers and consumers of television (see Keller and Stratyner 2005). Doing so reveals another strategy utilized by the network to broaden the audience to which it can market its promise of economic and cultural status through the acquisition of culinary capital.

By including the personal narratives of each contestant, most of which combine a desire to succeed with some form of family, personal, or professional need that would be alleviated by winning the $10,000 prize, *Chopped* balances the masculine impulse to compete with feminine attributes of identification and empathy. It is through this aspect of the show that it also makes its most overt gesture to class as the cash prize is framed as essential to the personal and/or professional transformation that the show promises its winner. Like in the cases of Deen and Lee, the acquisition of culinary capital is linked directly to financial gain as a crucial component of professional and personal success. At the same time, it can signal the complex interplay of class and race in relation to this transformative potential when non-white contestants stake their claim to culinary capital as a means of transcending the stereotypes and prejudices that are often evident in the hardships that inform their personal narratives. Finally, while competitive programming often includes a confrontational moment when expert judges critique and often eviscerate competitors who are deemed to be inadequate—for some shows, these climactic moments are essential, and judges like American Idol's Simon Cowell have achieved celebrity status for their bitter critiques—Chopped has a much less confrontational exchange in which judges often empathize with contestants and seek to help them learn from their experiences. While some judges are cast in the role of harsh "fathers" who discipline those contestants who don't "make the cut" and relegate them to the inevitable walk of shame, other judges assume a more maternal relationship to the contestants, establishing many of the same identifications that the show prompts between competitors and viewers.

Such balancing of a masculine competitiveness that pits contestants against each other with a feminine ethos of identification and care is also evident in the most recent iteration of Robert Irvine's Dinner: Impossible. Retitled Restaurant: Impossible, the show has been revamped to pit Irvine against seemingly insurmountable challenges not merely to measure his competitive muscle, but in the service of helping a failing restaurant. On the Food Network website, the show is summarized as follows:

> After combating countless "impossible dinners," Chef Robert Irvine faces a daunting new challenge: save America's most desperate restaurants from impending failure in just two days with only $10,000. In his new prime-time Food Network series, Restaurant: Impossible, Robert uses creativity and resourcefulness along with a lot of muscle in his fight to rescue these restaurants and give hope to the owners and their employees.

This rhetoric highlights how the show adapts certain aspects of the "challenge" that are proven techniques for drawing audiences to reality television while tempering the purely competitive aspect of Dinner: Impossible by heightening the show's emotional appeal. It does this by framing each challenge around the personal narrative of the restaurant owners, emphasizing the particular drama that has placed them in such a precarious position. While Irvine must still rely on his culinary "muscle" to intervene in these failing restaurants, this new format also allows him to show his heart as he—and his audiences—identify and empathize with these restaurant owners. At the dramatic conclusion of each show, Irvine and his audience are invited to share in the emotional catharsis experienced by the owners as their new and improved restaurants are revealed to them and then they open the doors to awaiting crowds. In the final moments of each episode, audiences are given brief updates that signal lasting change in the restaurants and their owners and prove once again Irvine's heroic ability to "save America's most desperate restaurants."

Despite the impulse to rescue America through masculine heroics, one of the Food Network's most popular initial forays into the realm of competitive programming was imported from Japan. Based on the Japanese cult sensation *Iron Chef*, *Iron Chef America* maintains its link to its Japanese roots, particularly as Iron Chef Masaharu Morimoto bridges the Japanese and American shows. As such, he, along with recently crowned Iron Chef Jose Garces, serves as one of the most visible non-white chefs on the network. Similarly, the "chairman," played by Hawaiian-born actor Mark Dacascos, takes on an air of otherness as he identifies as the nephew of Chairman Kaga from the Japanese series. However, rather than reading these elements of the show solely as an embrace of cultural and culinary difference, it is important to consider how the American version tames such otherness, including that which is communicated through many of the tropes that the show adopts from its Japanese counterpart. For example, gestures and sound effects that allude to classic kung fu movies are exaggerated in ways that make them comical. At the same time, while the show's "secret ingredient" can range from the mundane to the exotic, the vast majority of the show's cast, including the other Iron Chefs, competing chefs, and judges, reinforce whiteness as normative within foodie culture.

On other shows, white judges, including successful chefs, restaurateurs, and food industry insiders like Geoffrey Zakarian, Marc Murphy, Scott Conant, Alex Guarnaschelli, and Amanda Freitag, may be joined by a non-white judge like Marcus Samuelsson, Aarón Sanchez, or Maneet Chauhan. On the one hand, such inclusiveness can be read as the part of the network's effort to elide differences between white and non-white judges, contestants, and viewers. At the same time, subtle gestures often highlight the very otherness that is otherwise unacknowledged. Whether it is Aarón Sanchez explaining the taste and texture of an unfamiliar Mexican ingredient or Maneet Chauhan emphasizing the use of unusual spices, these non-white judges walk a fine line between sameness and difference, the familiar and the exotic, Self and Other.

In the end, shows like *Chopped* and *Restaurant: Impossible*, like the others that we have discussed in this chapter, emphasize the transformative power of cooking. This common theme is one aspect of televised food programming that connects it to the broader neoliberal project of utilizing personal lifestyle choices in the process of creating good citizens. From the contemporary woman who questions her ability to meet her domestic responsibilities to her family given limited time and money to the would-be star who challenges an Iron Chef and, in doing so, stakes his or her own claim to the culinary capital that comes from winning this battle, food programming from its inception to its most recent permutations has promised its viewers empowerment through food. Such productive power, however, ultimately serves to advance the broader project of circulating prevailing ideologies of gender and class to viewers who embrace and seek to emulate the lifestyles portrayed by their favorite celebrity chefs. As they seek their own share of the culinary capital that is required to achieve membership within a particular status group, these viewers demonstrate the subtle yet effective means through which televised food programming participates in the process of identity formation.

While the Food Network continually tweaks its programming as it negotiates an ever-changing landscape of gender and class, what remains constant is its ability to adapt itself in ways that allow it to continue offering culinary capital as both the catalyst and recompense for appropriate personal transformation. In fact, it may be this adaptability and flexibility that provides one explanation for televised food programming's longevity and popularity. Ultimately, such transformations remain illusory as this programming, like the meal assembly kitchens and e-grocers discussed in chapter 2, reinforces a range of gender- and class-based ideologies that constrain the possibilities for real social transformation.

–4–

Democratizing Taste?: Culinary Capital in the Digital Age

On February 24, 2003, renowned French chef Bernard Loiseau was found dead. According to news reports, Loiseau killed himself after his restaurant La Cote d'Or had its rating reduced to 17 from 19 out of 20 by the *Gault Millau*, France's most influential restaurant guide, and as rumors swirled that the restaurant was also about to lose one of its three Michelin stars. At the time of his death, Loiseau had built a culinary empire that included "three restaurants in Paris, Internet sites, a range of frozen dinners and a series of cookbooks" (Rose and Arkell 2003). While Loiseau's suicide exposes the culinary and financial pressures that come with this kind of success, it also speaks to the influence of top-tier restaurant guides and elite restaurant reviewers in conferring culinary capital upon those chefs and restaurants deemed worthy of their praise. In addition to the financial ramifications that would likely follow from a lower rating, Loiseau also risked losing his professional status as one of France's top chefs. In short, as a thriving chef, restaurateur, and entrepreneur, Loiseau had leveraged the culinary capital that came with his success to establish and maintain his professional and cultural identity. The erosion of one of the most important sources of that culinary capital, namely, the endorsement of the culinary elite, put Loiseau's reputation—and the empire that rested upon it—in jeopardy.

From this perspective, we read Loiseau's story as exemplifying how culinary capital circulates among the culinary elite, chefs and restaurateurs, and consumers. This process relies upon specific social hierarchies that grant authority to those deemed experts who are authorized to use their specialized knowledge and experience to determine when, why, and how culinary capital is to be given and taken away. "Modern economies are conscious of the necessity of deep, specialized knowledge for societal value creation, and the reorganization of social processes in a knowledge society is determined primarily by the availability and application of expert knowledge, whereby experts have a large impact as social actors in shaping the constitution of society" (Huber 1999, 5). From the knowledgeable staff at the meal assembly businesses that we discussed in chapter 2 to the Food Network's celebrity chefs and judges that we analyzed in chapter 3, experience and expertise play an important role in the circulation of culinary capital. This is also evident in the world of traditional restaurant criticism, which relies overtly on a notion of expertise that establishes the authority of the reviewers and, in doing so, positions them as arbiters of culinary capital. These critics are presumed to possess characteristics and knowledge that separate them from their readers and justify their authority to critique and recommend. As they do so, these restaurant critics, along with the publications that disseminate their expert opinions, regulate the transmission of culinary capital. They confer it upon those chefs who they deem worthy, and they make it accessible to consumers who accept their authority and rely upon their advice. From restaurant guides, newspaper reviews, and magazine articles to television and radio programs, the voices of culinary experts are easily accessible to those who value their opinions and seek their recommendations in order to establish their own credibility and acquire their own share of culinary capital.

FROM TRADITIONAL TO ONLINE RESTAURANT REVIEWING

The traditional approach to restaurant criticism fits perfectly within what Nikolas Rose identifies as the liberal model of governing, which is grounded upon "the language of obligation, duty and social citizenship" (Rose 1999, 166) and which confers authority upon the expert who, in turn, participates in the process of disciplining the citizenry: "It is experts who can tell us how we should conduct ourselves, not in the airy and vaporous moral nostrums, but as precise technologies for the care of the body, the care of others...and the conduct of our daily routines of life" (Rose 1999, 75). In this system, citizens are governed not merely by the oppressive regimes of the state, but also through their acceptance of the authority of a broad range of cultural experts who shape their behavior. However, in turning away from this model of traditional restaurant reviewing toward online reviews, contemporary culinary culture does not reject culinary capital; rather, it adapts it to a neoliberal model of self-governing that emphasizes individual freedom and choice. Rather than heralding this transition as a triumph of democracy as it allows individual opinions to circulate openly across the Internet and invites cyber-consumers to make their own decisions emancipated from the pressure to conform to the norms and standards established by the culinary elite, we argue that even as they emphasize their communal and participatory nature, these online sites simultaneously play a role in conferring culinary capital through a range of strategies for maintaining hierarchies of difference across this supposedly egalitarian landscape. At the same time, their claims about broad-based accessibility and participation, which are essential to their democratic impulses, warrant interrogation. Who does and who does not have access or choose to participate on these sites? How does frequent participation in such cyber-conversations signal its own form of class-based elitism that privileges individuals with the economic resources and leisure time to post reviews?

While this transition from traditional to online restaurant reviewing is ongoing and its consequences have not yet been fully realized, one bellwether of its impact upon the culinary scene came in November 2008 when renowned *New York* magazine restaurant critic Gael Greene was fired. In reporting this story in the *New York Times*, Glenn Collins characterizes debate over this firing among the "stomach-obsessed" as between two perspectives on Greene, either as "an arbiter of the evolution of American dining—a legend to whom respect must be paid—or a relic of a bygone era" (2008, D1). According to Adam Moss, *New York* magazine's editor in chief, the decision was a strictly financial one, explaining that Greene was laid off because "*New York* could no longer afford four food critics" (quoted in Collins 2008, D1). However, one could view this specific case through the lens of broader shifts in the publishing industry, in general, and restaurant reviewing and food-related reporting, in particular. Interestingly, one motivation for changes in both of these areas has been the impact of digital media on American culture. Paid experts like Greene are less in demand when new technologies enable laypeople to log on and sound off, thus seeming to render irrelevant the function of elite professional tastemakers and, perhaps, the culinary capital they simultaneously display and confer. At a time when people are dining out at unprecedented rates, "Americans have become more restaurant-savvy and less inclined to invest all of their dining-decision capital in the conclusions of one or two gastronomic gurus" (Frumkin 2007, 39), and new technologies make possible access to a broad range of opinions. As diners use these technologies to acquire knowledge for themselves as they make their own dining choices, we witness a transformation in how culinary capital is accessed by consumer citizens who continue to value it as a means of attaining privileged status.

This rise of new technology has fueled speculation about the demise of print journalism, and these predictions have gained increased credibility over the last few years as a host of newspapers and magazines have ceased publication or transitioned to primarily or exclusively online formats. Such decisions are framed, first and foremost, around shifts in how Americans access information and the financial implications of these changes. In asking if print journalism can perform its "traditional and normative Fourth Estate function in the information age" (2001, 96), Howard Tumber considers the nature and role of journalism in the face of changes in the production, distribution, and consumption of news. In discussing "web sites that promote participation rather than spectating" (2001, 102), he explains: "Some argue that the new electronic technologies are empowering citizens to participate in new democratic forums not only between government and the governed but also amongst citizens themselves. This communitarian view argues that the Internet is creating new 'virtual' as opposed to physical social formations providing a basis for a new politics and greater political participation by citizens" (2001, 101). Such a perspective raises crucial questions about the kinds of authority that have been circulated by print journalism and the future of a range of professional identities that it has helped to create and sustain. It also provides an important avenue for considering the relationship between modes of communication and the forms of capital, including culinary capital, that are transmitted by them.

As a first step in doing so, we utilize Herbert Gans's distinction between "everyday newsworkers" and "professional journalists," acknowledging that the appearance of everyday news on the Internet (via blogs, listservs, streaming video sites, and so on) allows everyday newsworkers to reach the kinds of remote audiences previously reached only by professionals (2007, 162). In outlining the similarities and differences between everyday newsworkers and professional journalists, Gans highlights the facts that the former "mix facts and opinions without making the distinction" and that they "are not hierarchically organized and, as a result, benefit from more egalitarian working conditions than professional journalists" (2007, 164).

As Gans recognizes, professional journalism depends upon a notion of expertise through which reporters and journalists acquire credibility and authority. These professional identities are constructed and maintained within a broader system that includes formal news organizations, a management network of media owners and producers, and the consumers to whom they market their publications and products. Clearly, this model aligns with what Rose identifies as the liberal framework that relies upon specific hierarchies of authority through which citizens are governed. Across the cultural landscape, experts are granted such authority due to their specialized knowledge, skills, and experiences. For example, Glenn Collins describes Gael Greene as "the priestess of radicchio, beurre blanc and arugula" (2008). He quotes Robert Lape, restaurant critic for *Crain's New York Business*, who said that Ms. Greene's "palate is one of the best in the business," and that "she could always parse a meal quite brilliantly, and her skills have not diminished" (quoted in G. Collins 2008, D1). Like all credible traditional restaurant critics, Greene may share with her readers a love of good food and a passion for fine dining; however, her status as culinarily capitalized depends more upon differentiation than similarity even as her readers seek their own claim to such capitalization by accepting her expert opinions. As her dismissal from *New York* magazine suggests, there has been a crucial shift across the culinary landscape in how such status, credibility, and authority are acquired that is characterized by claims of democratization like those espoused by online restaurant review sites. Now that laypeople have become accustomed to being asked for their opinions, including giving customer feedback to businesses, texting or emailing comments or votes to television programs, judging reality shows, and so on (Skidelsky 2005, 14), the surge of amateur criticism on the Internet makes elite differentiation seem quaint—at least at first.

At one level, it is true that traditional hierarchies—of writer over reader; expert over novice; critic over consumer—are disrupted in the digital age in ways that are often characterized as movements toward democratization. Why accept passively the opinions of news anchors and newspaper editors when viewers and readers can express and circulate their own views via websites and blogs? Why rely upon the recommendations of professional restaurant critics when diners can share their own experiences and access the opinions of fellow "foodies"? To use Tumber's (2001) terminology, why "spectate" when one can participate? In short, the rise of digital media marks a shift not only in how most Americans access information, but also in how they relate to and participate in processes for creating and circulating it. These changes impact not only the flow of information and the ways in which authority is granted to those who participate in this process, but also the very terms and conditions by which judgments are made and value is determined, as evidenced by the contested concepts of "authenticity" and "taste" that we discuss below.

Although digital media do allow for a dramatic expansion in the number of people who can participate in this process and the ways in which they can do so, we resist the temptation to celebrate this change as an all-inclusive triumph of democracy. As longtime *Village Voice* restaurant critic Robert Sietsema explains, "As with many things on the Web, this profusion of voices is often touted as a wondrous blow for democracy, a long-overdue rising up of the masses against the elitist overlords of the culinary realm" (2010). However, he cautions us about what we lose in the trade-off: "I'm all for everyone having his or her say, but when it comes to cultural criticism there is a strong case to be made for professionalism and expertise" (Sietsema 2010). In short, Sietsema is wary about the quality of the opinions that proliferate on the Internet in contrast to the voices of reason he thinks prevail in traditional publications.

Alice Marwick offers a different perspective on the question of how we should assess the libratory potential of digital media in her analysis of the discourses of democracy and egalitarianism that have framed critical and popular responses to YouTube: "I am highly suspicious of rhetorics of 'democracy' that posit YouTube as an alternative to the limits of traditional political participation. These rhetorics ignore the limited avenues of participation available to users and the firm authority of the site's corporate ownership, particularly with regard to profit-driven decision-making. Furthermore, claims of 'egalitarianism' do not take into account the power relations *within* communities that function to privilege certain subject positions over others, as well as unequal access to Internet technologies in the first place. While it is easy to fall into the trap of positing new technologies as utopian and revolutionary, it is ultimately unfruitful" (Marwick 2007, 31). Similarly, this chapter's examination of online restaurant review sites demonstrates that while a cultural shift toward digital media as source of information and site for participatory engagement does initiate significant changes in *how* culinary capital circulates, it does not mark its demise. Instead, we read it as signaling a change in how culinary capital is produced in relation to shifting expectations of expertise and accessibility.

THE RISE OF ONLINE RESTAURANT REVIEW SITES

In both their marketing and their practices, online restaurant review sites shun traditional culinary hierarchies and privilege user-based fora that create virtual communities.[1] In doing so, they seek to distance themselves from culinary elitism and stake their claim to a more participatory and, presumably, democratic impulse. Visitors to Chowhound.com, for example, can find these sentiments expressed clearly in its "Chowhound Manifesto," which reads, in part:

> No media outlets serve Chowhounds. They've never had a place to gather and exchange information. This discerning, passionate crowd has long been completely invisible and utterly disenfranchised ... until now.
>
> If you, too, fret endlessly about making every bite count; if you'd grow weak from hunger rather than willingly eat something less than delicious, this place is for you! Welcome to our community. Let's talk. Let's swap tips.
>
> You needn't be an expert to participate. If you're less food-obsessed than the rest of us, but have a yen for egg creams, gazpacho, or Quisp Cereal, let the resident hounds guide you to the best stuff. Follow (and chime in on) the rollicking discussion—featuring thousands of messages from characters all over the world.

It is important to note how this manifesto emphasizes the site's inclusiveness as chowhounds welcome experts and amateurs alike to join their community. Even those without culinary expertise are invited not only to "follow" but to "chime in on" the discussions. Clearly, this community identifies itself not as one in which those in the know use their authority to direct the choices and actions of others but rather, as one where all community members share information and opinions openly and honestly so that each person can make his or her own decisions. At the same time, one need only imagine the motives of users for looking up restaurant reviews, as opposed to mere menus and coordinates—the desire to tap into the elite knowledge of experts and tastemakers—to be skeptical about the site's claims to democratization.

This same framework is evidenced on Dine.com, which underscores the democratic and participatory nature of its endeavor. In assuring readers that all posted restaurant reviews are unbiased and come from visitors to the site rather than from paid reviewers, Dine distances itself from the traditional hierarchy that privileges the views and opinions of expert reviewer over amateur consumer. It furthers this goal by constructing a history in which site founder Andrew Condru started asking his friends for restaurant recommendations when he found himself "uninspired by traditional reviews in the local papers." In explaining how the site works, Dine also emphasizes the importance of active participation by its readers. In establishing their profiles, members create "hotlists" of favorite restaurants that allow Dine to make specific recommendations based on each member's particular tastes. It also uses these profiles to identify members with common restaurants on their respective lists and who, presumably, have similar tastes. Individual participation enhances the communal experience just as individual choices are buoyed by community support: "What this means is that by playing an active role in Dine (e.g., posting reviews and listing your favorite restaurants), you are simultaneously improving the quality of the site for everyone! This, to us, reflects the true power of the web." Given their missions and purposes, both Chowhound and Dine rely upon individuals being "*active* in making choices in order to further their own interests" (Rose 1999, 142). At the same time, these presumably personal interests merge with those of the websites as users are invited to share them with each other, thus generating the websites' content and keeping them current and interactive. However, as these sites monitor, record, and use individuals' choices for future marketing, they can be linked to the e-grocers we discussed in chapter 2 who maintain user profiles that track selections, compile data, anticipate behavior, and attempt to influence future choices. In both cases, the acquisition of culinary capital requires making one's private choices publicly accessible, thus ensuring that these individual decisions are informed by the values and priorities of one's real and/or virtual communities.

This emphasis on the active participation of Chowhound users also informs how Jim Leff, the site's founder, responds to criticisms about the site. A June 2007 post by CapeCodBob, for example, laments the site's focus on fine dining, viewing it as a sign of its shift away from its core "chowhound" principles: "It's even gone to the point where posts for good food in Maine, get replies about fine dining with nary a mention about the best crab roll, or baked beans or codfish cake or blueberry pancakes. Anyone who goes to Maine in late summer and has ANY dessert other than blueberry or raspberry pie ought to be dismissed from chowhound.com. Please, please, please. Would you foodies go to one of the gazillion sites dedicated to overpriced mélange of decorated foods and let us have our chow back?" CapeCodBob has clearly framed his criticism around a distinction between "chowhounds" and "foodies" that belies the site's claims to inclusiveness and serves as an indication that the site's democratic philosophy is not so easily put into practice.

However, in responding to this criticism, Jim Leff reiterates the egalitarian impulse upon which the site was founded: "If you feel the mix is skewing one way or the other on a particular board, it's really important to bear in mind that Chowhound is not like a tv or radio station, where a set program is imposed on you. The site's what you make of it." Leff's juxtaposition of television and radio viewers and listeners who have set programming "imposed" upon them and Chowhound users who have the ability to direct discussion and, thus, shape the site's overall content and direction, mimics the distinction between passive consumers who look to the traditional restaurant critic for expert advice and online restaurant review site enthusiasts who find their own opinions welcome and who take an active role in generating discussion. On Chowhound, Leff asserts, the power lies not with a few experts who determine the site's content but, rather, in the hands of all users who are invited to make the site whatever they want it to be.

This logic fits squarely with a broader claim about the democratizing influence of the Internet as it allows "regular people" to voice their opinions, share their views, and connect with each other free from the mediation imposed by traditional media. While CapeCodBob seeks to police the Chowhound site by excluding those participants he deems inauthentic, Leff's position is that the task of shaping the Chowhound community is shared by all of its members. It is essentially democratic as the voices of those who choose to actively participate in the community determine the site's content and direction. Nonetheless, this debate, in and of itself, suggests that the site's broad egalitarian impulse is not so easily enacted. At the same time, it indicates one important consequence that this democratic impulse has had on one of the key barometers for making culinary judgments, namely the concept of "authenticity." Within this new framework, what are the criteria by which "authenticity" is to be determined, and who, ultimately, becomes the arbiter of such decisions? While Jim Leff does not want to assume the authority to delineate between "authentic" and "inauthentic" chowhounds, CapeCodBob has no problem asserting such distinctions and, presumably, claiming the authority to define these categories for himself. One cannot help but reflect that this very conversation is a performance of culinary capital by both contributors, as the act of dabbling online suggests plentiful leisure time and access to the resources that would inform their knowledge.

While Chowhound is deeply invested in differentiating itself from the hierarchical model of traditional restaurant criticism by emphasizing its member-based community, this exchange between CapeCodBob and Jim Leff demonstrates how a term like "authenticity" can be contested openly within this democratic framework, thus raising questions of authority that undermine this effort at democratization. Rather than being exceptional, such debates occur frequently on the site's discussion boards, revealing the extent to which the site establishes its own set of hierarchies and utilizes culinary capital to do so, even as it shifts the terms upon which this process is enacted. Although Leff makes broad claims for the inclusiveness of the website in his response to the criticism raised by CapeCodBob, debates about who is and who is not an "authentic" chowhound run rampant across the site's discussion boards, revealing the difficulty with sustaining the open community that Leff imagines.

Despite this democratic narrative that claims that active participation by its users creates an open and egalitarian community, we argue that Chowhound adapts rather than rejects a model in which the promise of culinary capital is framed around notions of difference and exclusivity. To understand how this is done, we return to the concept of "omnivorousness" that we discussed in chapter 1. In considering how late-twentieth-century capitalism has adapted the process by which economic and social distinction is attained through the acquisition of valued commodities, Warde, Martens, and Olsen (1999, 107) argue that such class-based distinctions are on the wane and that given the onslaught of such commodities, "appreciation of a much wider variety of cultural genres—dubbed 'omnivorousness'—is spreading, if somewhat unevenly, replacing snobbish attitudes with a comparatively benevolent and tolerant pluralism." While omnivorousness may initially be read as a gesture toward democratization as it promotes fluidity across the spectrum of high and lowbrow tastes, Warde et al. maintain that "it is itself exclusionary, a form of cultural symbolism, perhaps exhibiting a qualified cultural tolerance but with a significant, if residual, class basis" (1999, 107). In other words, while omnivorousness, which is about being open to liking everything, may be contrasted with the exclusionary impulse of snobbishness, this "tolerance," itself, can be read as an elite class signifier.

This concept of omnivorousness provides an alternative method for establishing distinctions within a supposedly democratic system that emphasizes individual freedom and choice. As individuals find themselves "free in the sphere of consumption" (Warde et al. 1999, 120), particular choices take on added significance as a means of establishing and maintaining one's identity. Consequently, "misconceived aesthetic decisions will convey regrettable and damaging messages about the self. Hence, anxiety is associated with choice" (Warde et al. 1999, 120). This anxiety is heightened by an ever-expanding economy of consumption and an ever-increasing variety of commodities from which to choose. Against this backdrop, the emphasis shifts from the selectivity of one's choices to omnivorousness, which emphasizes "extend[ing] knowledge and familiarity of as many items as possible and advanc[ing] the claim that refinement is to be identified through breadth of experience or awareness" (Warde et al. 1999, 120). What becomes a mark of distinction, in other words, is not the exclusiveness of one's tastes or choices but, rather, that individual's openness to a range of experiences that cut across familiar boundaries—including those of class, race, and ethnicity—through which distinct identities have traditionally been established. In short, those who seek out the greatest variety of tastes and who are open to the broadest range of experiences emerge as the most culturally capitalized. Using this framework, we can understand how online review sites that attempt to distinguish themselves from their traditional counterparts by emphasizing their democratic impulse nonetheless establish various modes of differentiation as they assume their own role in the circulation of privileged versions of culinary capital.

SEPARATING CHOWHOUNDS FROM FOODIES

Even as Chowhound emphasizes its inclusiveness, its discussion boards reveal a contradiction between its democratic philosophy and its everyday practices. While all may be invited to participate, not all participation is necessarily equal. While the cracks in its egalitarian façade are evident in the debate between CapeCodBob and Jim Leff over "authentic" and "inauthentic" chowhounds, they can be traced back to another part of the Chowhound manifesto, which reads: "Chowhounds know where the good stuff is, and they never settle for less than optimal deliciousness, whether dining in splendor or grabbing a quick slice. We're not talking about foodies. Foodies eat where they're told. Chowhounds blaze trails. They comb through neighborhoods for culinary treasure. They despise hype. And while they appreciate ambiance and service, they can't be fooled by flash." This distinction between chowhounds and foodies, which is crucial for establishing the site's identity, depends on the presumption that chowhounds, due in part to their omnivorousness, are "authentic" players on the contemporary food scene while foodies, with their inclination toward elitism, are "inauthentic" as they privilege conformity in their pursuit of culinary status. A chowhound's fundamental goal is "optimal deliciousness," wherever it appears across the culinary landscape—"whether dining in splendor or grabbing a quick slice." True chowhounds are identifiable not by the exclusivity of their culinary choices but, rather, by the vast range of their tastes and culinary experiences. They embrace the full breadth of their culinary options while foodies, presumably anxious about appearing to make the "wrong" choices, would rather follow those who they deem to be in the know. From this perspective, "authenticity" is marked by the omnivorousness of chowhounds while foodies, who continue to embrace an elitist model in which they imitate choices made by others, are labeled "inauthentic."

With a manifesto that immediately separates the "authentic" chowhound from the "inauthentic" foodie, it is not surprising that this distinction becomes an important part of establishing and maintaining the credibility of the site and the culinary capital that it offers its users. The criteria upon which this distinction is based also expose assumptions about class and taste that are aimed at dismissing foodies as those who are more likely to follow passively the recommendations of traditional food critics, seek out the most popular or trendy restaurants, and emphasize style over substance, atmosphere over quality, presentation over preparation, hype over taste. Beyond Chowhound's manifesto, in which chowhounds are immediately distanced from rank-and-file foodies who "eat where they're told," the site's Frequently Asked Questions (FAQ) page further elucidates this distinction as it seeks to define a chowhound: "A Chowhound is someone who spends nearly every waking moment planning her or his next meal. Whether eating in a white-tablecloth restaurant or grabbing takeout on the way to work, Chowhounds hate to ingest anything undelicious. They won't hesitate to go far, far out of their way for even slightly better." Once again, chowhounds are identified by their omnivorousness as they seek out "deliciousness" across the culinary landscape—even if it takes them "far, far out of their way." In contrast, the FAQ tells us: "Foodies eat what they're told. They lap up hype about the 'hot' new restaurant/cookbook/ingredient. They'll explore unfamiliar neighborhoods, but only with their *Zagat* securely in hand. Chowhounds spurn established opinion to sniff out their own secret deliciousness. The places they find today will show up in newspapers two years from now and in *Zagat* in four, by which time they'll undoubtedly have grown crowded and overpriced." Chowhounds are trailblazers, trendsetters, tastemakers; they are empowered subjects on a "quest for self-realization" (Rose 1999, 142). To some extent, their contempt for foodies is a function of their presumed passivity as they rely on traditional restaurant reviews "with their *Zagat* securely in hand."[2] This can also be read as a distain for foodies' anxiety in the face of an ever-increasing range of culinary options. While chowhounds embrace these seemingly endless choices, foodies are intimidated by them. In short, foodies are followers; chowhounds are leaders. Foodies seek culinary capital by mimicking the choices and opinions of those deemed experts and by following culinary trends; chowhounds acquire culinary capital by rejecting the exclusivity that informs the choices of the culinary elite and staking their claim to a full range of culinary experiences. In doing so, they deem themselves more democratic and "authentic" participants in the contemporary food scene (Johnston and Baumann 2010, 55); however, this identification must be problematized as chowhounds construct their communal identity through familiar strategies of differentiation that conflict with their democratic and egalitarian aspirations.

As Bourdieu explains, "tastes (i.e., manifested preferences) are the practical affirmation of an inevitable difference. It is no accident that, when they have to be justified, they are asserted purely negatively, by the refusal of other tastes" (1984, 56). While the concept of omnivorousness embraced by chowhounds might at first be read as challenging an understanding of "taste" that necessitates some form of selectivity, a slightly modified concept of "taste" does allow chowhounds to differentiate themselves from the elitism that they attribute to foodies. In distinguishing omnivorous tastes that are deemed authentic from elitist tastes that are deemed inauthentic, chowhounds utilize the "discursive and affective aspects of food" to "negotiate the parameters of 'culinary citizenship,' a form of affective citizenship which grants subjects the ability to claim and inhabit certain subject positions via their relationship to food" (Mannur 2007, 13). The chowhound community, in other words, embraces its omnivorous tastes as constitutive of its identity and, therefore, a requirement for those who stake a claim to authenticity within the contemporary culinary scene. In short, foodies need not apply.

It is also important to recognize that although the concepts of "authenticity" and "taste" as embraced by chowhounds to distinguish between themselves and foodies do not make overt reference to class, they are nonetheless fraught with class-based connotations. Sharon Zukin argues that we can only recognize spaces as authentic once we have achieved the mobility to examine them from the outside—from a distance that reflects, in this case, upward class mobility (2008, 728). The more connected we are to the inner workings of the space, the less likely we are to call it "authentic"—it just is what it is. Authentic has something to do with being traditional, being apart from "the standardized realm of mass consumption" (Zukin 2008, 736), a feat more easily accomplished by those outsiders with capital than those without it.

This becomes more apparent when chowhounds emphasize their anti-elitist impulses. Specifically, in framing this issue, the website takes pains to clarify that chowhounds are not merely cheap eaters but, instead, are savvy enough to reject the notion that authentic culinary experiences must come with a hefty price tag. Johnston and Baumann note that what one consumes is less important in foodie discourse than the "disposition one brings to food—as a subject for study, aesthetic appreciation and knowledge acquisition" (2010, 57). Rather than assuming that culinary capital comes from imitating the upper-class tendency to limit choices and seek out only the most exclusive culinary experiences, chowhounds stake their own claim to culinary capital by nurturing an "appreciation of a much wider variety of cultural genres" and replacing "snobbish attitudes with a comparatively benevolent and tolerant pluralism" (Warde et al. 1999, 107). In doing so, the website does assign exclusive knowledge to chowhounds, namely, their sense of value and their ability to balance quality and cost: "Chowhounds go way out of their way to find good food at any price. They're savvy enough to appreciate value. Why buy rugalach at Balducci's when it's available at the baker's outlet in Brooklyn at a fraction of the cost? But they also know certain pleasures come at a price—foie gras ain't cheap, and Château Margaux is one terrific drink. No pleasure is gladly missed." Chowhounds resist the idea that four-star restaurants serve the best food, arguing that diners have been brainwashed by "media and commercial interests" into believing this. Because Chowhound was built for the express purpose of "be[ing] a grass-roots alternative to traditional media," it exemplifies how the process for acquiring culinary capital transitions from a hierarchical one in which culinary experts confer it upon those who accept their authority and mimic their tastes to an egalitarian model in which supposedly free individuals take an active role in forming more "authentic" tastes, in part by availing themselves of the full range of culinary options and experiences.

From this perspective, it is clear why discussions about the differences between chowhounds and foodies that permeate the website's boards are often framed by the concept of "taste," with particular emphasis on when taste-based distinctions may be deemed "authentic" and when they should be dismissed as "inauthentic." The class-based element to this discussion is apparent, especially when chowhounds debate the relationship among price, quality, and authenticity. Grubber4, for example, insinuates that chowhounds' anti-elitist impulse can go too far, including when posters privilege cheap food over expensive cuisine merely to promote this aspect of chowhound identity. He writes: "When someone wants contemporary Vietnamese on the SF Bay Board, they are quickly persuaded to skip the higher end contemporary restaurants and ridiculed for not considering pho houses as an alternative. I can't tell you how many times people have posted to go to Bodega Bistro instead of the Slanted Door if they want 'authentic' Vietnamese cuisine...The recommendation to go there is purely price driven and that lower price has deluded the posters into thinking it's preferable. Lower end, cheap whole [sic] in the walls are fine, but when they are compared to classic eateries more favorably, it's a joke." In this case, Grubber4 criticizes those who would unquestionably locate authenticity in "lower end, cheap whole [sic] in the walls" and who would dismiss "higher end contemporary restaurants" presumably based not on the relative quality of their food but, rather, out of a desire to resist buying into a class-based hierarchy. Grubber4's post can also be read as challenging the omnivorous nature of the chowhound identity, exposing the fact that in emphasizing the broadest possible range of tastes and choices, this identity contradicts the fundamental purpose of the site; namely, to advise users which culinary experiences should be avoided.

While some posters echo Grubber4's concerns, others focus on the egalitarian impulse that is at the heart of chowhound's manifesto. Steve writes that "if you do recommend anything less than a Temple of Gastronomy for someone's birthday or anniversary, that is invariably derided." Gary Soup elaborated on this point: "It's become an elite vetting service, and an outsider casually browsing the SF Boards over a period of time could easily be left with the impression that there are only a score or so of sit-down restaurants that are worth spending one's money on, and once someone has typed up and printed out the foodie 'A' list there's no need to look any deeper. Chowhound is becoming more and more like a Wednesday night tent meeting." For Steve and Gary Soup, those who focus only on high-end restaurants threaten to shift the site toward an elitist foodie philosophy that privileges the trendy over the truly delicious and focuses more on atmosphere and price (i.e., high class) than on the quality of the food. While others accept this criticism, they also defend the right of all posters to share their opinions, acknowledging that while they may not be able to afford such high-end dining, they appreciate the range and diversity of recommendations. Glencora writes, "I still enjoy reading, though, and have learned a lot. I just have to force myself to accept the fact that I'm never going to have the ten-dollar burger or twelve-buck sandwich that everyone says is so great." Adrienne156 expresses a similar sentiment: "I don't know if me being on this site for only a year makes me too new, but the wealth of knowledge I've found on here makes CH an absolutely priceless resource."

Taste is polysemic in these discussions; its meaning alternates between a predilection for the expensive and established on the one hand, and a desire for the authentic and the unknown on the other. In some cases, it serves as a mark of distinction when framed through the discourses of exclusivity and elitism; in other instances, it contributes to establishing an identity marked by openness to an ever-expanding range of culinary choices. It is invoked in the effort to dismiss foodies as snobs who unequivocally champion expensive restaurants and to extol chowhounds for their willingness to spurn the expensive in favor of the harder-to-find or more esoteric. In short, "taste" can be defined in ways that support the privilege that is assumed to come with affluence; on the other hand, it can seem to challenge such established elitism as it values omnivorousness over exclusion. Despite Jim Leff's hope that these sensibilities can and should peacefully coexist—even within the same chowhound—the boards tell another story, a story about a battle for culinary capital.

The chowhounds themselves are fully aware of the battle, and comment on it with some fluency. Uptown Jimmy writes:

> I've been around since the earlier days, and you are absolutely correct. The massive influx of newer Hounds in the last few years has considerably diluted the overall quality and reliability of advice on the site, IMHO. There is better luck to be had on certain boards, for sure, but I've seen some absolutely awful advice posted on the South board many times, people absolutely raving about restaurants that

are mediocre at best, or even barely edible, by the standards of any true Hound. It's not a total decline by any means, but I think most old-school Hounds would never in a million years have imagined that there would come a time when a whole section of the site would be devoted to chain restaurants, where, by the way, a discussion is currently ongoing concerning the relative merits of Applebee's and Chili's. I've actually seen numerous posters loudly accuse those of us who avoid chain restaurants as having some sort of arrogant bias against them, as if chain-ness or popularity is the innate problem for us, not the generally crap-tacular food or the obesity that usually accompanies the patronage of such places.

In this context, "taste" emerges not as a means of distinguishing chow-hounds from foodies but, rather, for separating "true" chowhounds (i.e., those who can trace their lineage back to the website's beginning) from "false" chowhounds (i.e., those newcomers who seem to dilute the chowhound phil-osophy). "Taste" is taken here to be objective and universal among "true" chowhounds and serves as the basis for deriding those "false" chowhounds who embrace chains like Applebee's and Chili's. Uptown Jimmy embodies the perspective that relies upon an elitist differentiation between "real" versus "chain" restaurants to establish its credibility. However, he resists such iden-tification by justifying his disdain for chain restaurants based not upon an "ar-rogant bias against them" but rather upon the poor quality of their food and the negative health consequences that he assumes come with patronizing them. Uptown Jimmy's comments thus resonate with Sharon Zukin's obser-vation that "sometimes the consumption practices of an existing community repel new residents, who are turned off by old timers' social class or race, or by the way their bodies consume public space. Authenticity, then, becomes an effective means for new residents to cleanse and claim space; since it is they and the media for which many of them work who define the term, it reflects their own self-interest" (2008, 745). New residents are "united by their con-sumption of authenticity. And, over time, this norm of alternative consumption becomes a means of excluding others from their space" (Zukin 2008, 745). Although Uptown Jimmy aligns his own identity with that of the "old-school Chowhound" and imagines the chain-restaurant lovers as the new interlopers on the block, his rebuke of the "obesity that usually accompanies the patron-age of such places" suggests a concern for the way non-elite bodies con-sume not only public space, but also food. In setting himself apart from the fat chain-loving masses who have "diluted" the conversation, Uptown Jimmy implicitly sets forth his own taste for something presumably better than "crap-tacular" chain food as distinct; he is culinarily capitalized. This concern for health, couched in disdain for the body size of chain restaurant customers, appears to be a commonly acceptable framework for articulating what are really class-based biases (LeBesco 2004).

More diplomatic posters use their posts not to reinforce their own status as culinarily capitalized, but rather to advocate for peaceful coexistence of the warring taste factions. In responding to posts by CapeCodBob, Hungry Pangolin posts "CCB complains that CH [Chowhound] has become too foodie, whereas someone agrees that CH has gone downhill because it has become too populist. I'd say that that's evidence that CH is encompassing a greater spectrum...all to the good." Likewise, ALopez asserts: "I have noticed bit of a swing toward the high end on the DC board. I think that's fine since some posters seem to really be into that. What I don't like is that those posts seem much more likely to bring out the over-the-top, citysearch-style drive-by-rant by one-time posters. And they tend to digress into pointless chatter over who has a more educated palate, or who understands what the chef is trying to do, or whatever. Those discussions almost invariably get nasty. More importantly, they don't help anyone eat better. So why do it?" In chiding posters for getting into pointless squabbles over taste, ALopez does not choose sides. Interestingly, though, he sets up Chowhound as a distinct site for the articulation of taste, unlike what happens on Citysearch. At the same time, his criticism of "pointless chatter over who has a more educated palate" counters Robert Lape's celebration of Gael Greene's palate as "one of the best in the business" (quoted in G. Collins 2008, D1), suggesting that some chowhounds adopt the very elitism shunned by the Chowhound Manifesto.

Ultimately, the transition from print-based to online restaurant reviews reveals a broader reframing of the concepts of "authenticity" and "taste" in light of the shift toward democracy and egalitarianism that is presumed to accompany the rise of digital media. Traditional restaurant reviews used these terms in ways that allowed those "foodies" with economic capital to stake their claim to broader cultural capital, including culinary capital, as their tastes were deemed most authentic, their choices were presumed to be correct, and, consequently, they were deemed worthy of imitation (Johnston and Baumann 2010). Those with less economic and cultural capital were expected to defer to those to whom it had been granted by mimicking the elitism that informed their choices. However, such an overtly hierarchical model has been disrupted as presumably free individuals use the Internet to stake their own claim to active participation in their culture; in doing so, they contest the entitlement of the elite to define notions of "authenticity" and "taste" and to use them as a means of limiting individual choices. At the same time, these individuals stake their own claims to "authenticity" and "taste" in establishing new hierarchies—chowhounds vs. foodies; "true" vs. "false" chowhounds—across this supposedly egalitarian landscape.

This analysis reveals that while the transition from traditional, print-based restaurant reviews to online restaurant reviews marks an important shift in how culinary capital circulates, it does not signal its demise. To the contrary, culinary capital proves to be an especially adept tool for negotiating this transition as it moves equally well across the hierarchical model of traditional restaurant criticism and the democratic model of online reviews. While this transition may initially disrupt the class-based assumptions about "authenticity" and "taste" that sustained the traditional model, the online communities that emerge from this process are not immune from these issues or the debates they engender. In fact, they are deeply implicated in the processes through which those who have the economic and cultural capital—including the leisure time, the culinary knowledge, and the economic resources to dine out on a regular basis—to participate in such online discussions are separated from those who do not. Ultimately, this reinforces rather than weakens economic and social hierarchies while revealing the role of culinary capital in sustaining them. If French chef Bernard Loiseau succumbed to a system that bestowed culinary capital upon him and then threatened to take it away, are the posters on Chowhound engaging in a significantly different process as they separate themselves from foodies and, in doing so, stake their own claim to culinary capital? In the end, this chapter makes clear that through the proliferation and democratization of expertise illustrated by the rise of online opportunities for restaurant criticism, culinary capital meshes seamlessly with projects of the self.

Culinary Resistance: State Fairs, Competitive Eating, and "Junk" Foodies

In a video montage posted on YouTube, visitors to the 2006 Minnesota State Fair identify many of the fifty-nine food items that are available on a stick. The list ranges from familiar items like beef and chicken kabobs, steak, lamb, pork chops to more exotic selections like alligator, porcupine meatballs, and teriyaki ostrich. It includes pepperoni pizza and spaghetti on a stick, a variety of corn dogs, and, of course, countless sweets, including cotton candy, caramel apples, chocolate-covered cheesecake, pecan pie, and deep-fried Twinkies, Three Musketeers, Milky Ways, and Snickers. While the Minnesota State Fair continues to play up its "everything on a stick" gimmick, its menu options are not unique; rather, many of these items would be familiar to regular visitors to most state fairs and carnivals. Such a menu reflects an apparent celebration of "unhealthy" or "excessive" eating that is promoted not only at state fairs and carnivals, but also at the other sites that we analyze in this chapter, namely competitive eating contests and "junk" food websites and blogs. While these sites can be read as resisting the privileged eating practices that promise culinary capital to those individuals who adhere to them, they must also be recognized as trafficking in their own form of culinary capital, once again signaling its variety and adaptability across the cultural landscape. More specifically, while some of the sites we discuss in this chapter subvert the usual criteria for culinary capital, they would not find entirely alien the practice of accumulating power or status based on one's foodways. As such, even sites of resistance to privileged food discourses engage with culinary capital, but award it based on different, arguably subversive food practices and knowledges.

In turning to an examination of cultural sites that promote culinary practices that seem to run counter to the privileged attitudes and assumptions about food and foodways that we discussed in chapter 1, we consider what is at stake when individuals make isolated food choices or adopt long-term dietary practices that conflict with the broader field against which these choices are negotiated. Specifically, as contemporary upwardly mobile middle-class American society buys into a food culture that privileges sustainability, health, and dietary restraint, as evidenced by the backlash against industrial foods, the growing emphasis on and availability of natural and organic products, and the panic over weight, body size, and the obesity epidemic, we focus on the strong counter-current that resists these discourses and derives pleasure from indulging in "bad" food practices. If such behavior marks a departure from a particular path to culinary capital and a challenge to the cultural authority through which it is privileged, then we must consider the possibility that those who engage in eating habits and practices that run contrary to their society's prevailing expectations liberate themselves from the regulatory power of culinary capital. On the other hand, we must also consider another possibility; namely, that their behavior marks an ironic embrace of culinary capital by those who seem, on the surface at least, uninterested in it or the status that it can confer. This chapter addresses these questions through an analysis of what we identify as "sites of resistance" that celebrate eating practices that run contrary to privileged culinary trends and expectations, concluding that they function ultimately to amplify the role of culinary capital even as they assume a complicated stance toward it.

ESCAPISM, EXCESS, AND FAIR FARE

It is certainly not difficult to identify state fairs and carnivals as sites at which the mandate for a controlled diet based on healthy food choices is at least temporarily suspended. After all, fairs and carnivals happen during leisure time—time taken off from work and production and dedicated instead to consumption. However, "there is a continuity and a dialectic between everyday activities and these heightened events" (Abrahams and Bauman 1977, 100). Tensions between restraint and excess, between healthiness and indulgence, then, are not limited to the fair, but rather reflect and inform culinary and dietary practices in everyday life. Evident in foodways at the fair are what Alessandro Falassi has called rites of conspicuous consumption involving abundant and excessive yet solemnly consumed food and drink, and rites of reversal in which "significant terms which are in binary opposition in the 'normal' life of a culture"—like good food and bad food—"are inverted" (1987, 4). As visitors wander up and down rows of food vendors offering any number of deep-fried, jumbo-sized, calorie-packed snacks, cultural expectations to make healthy food choices or to refrain from excessive eating seem to disappear and along with them any promise of culinary capital that comes from adhering to such mandates.

While fruits and vegetables are on display in the judging pavilions, where ribbons adorn each year's award-winning entries, there are very few to be found in the surrounding food courts unless, of course, they are battered, buttered, deep fried, and/or chocolate covered. Indeed, in the commercial food space of the fair, most of the providers are oriented toward profit, selling what the people want during the fair—a limited assortment of greasy or sugary offerings—rather than being linked in any coherent way to the community as are the foods in the judging pavilions, where one merely ogles the enormous pumpkins or stunning tomatoes, rather than eating them. This tension between businesses motivated by the profit that comes from selling consumers the unhealthy foods that they want and a community that seeks to promote the health and well-being of its citizens plays itself out across the fairgrounds, signaling a complex and contradictory engagement with culinary capital.

While there can be any number of other attractions to lure visitors—from carnival rides to musical performances, from prize-winning farm animals to monster truck races, from celebrations of local history and folklore to family-oriented games and activities—food cannot be overlooked as a main attraction. More specifically, interviews conducted over several days with visitors to the 2009 Indiana State Fair reveal the extent to which the freedom to indulge in "excessive" or "unhealthy" eating that is promoted at the fair played a significant role in their decision to attend this event.[1] Michael and Meg, for example, who were enjoying their barbecued chicken and pizza and anticipating some funnel cake, elephant ears, and fried desserts, said that they "look forward to coming for the food." Curtis, who was eating an Italian sausage sandwich and French fries and who also expected to enjoy some funnel cake and elephant ears, said that food was one of the event's main perks, that it was part of "the thrill of the fair." Eric and Jane were excited to enjoy "food that you don't get anywhere else," and David said that he and his family came to this fair mainly for the food and he shared his experiences at several other state fairs, including the Wisconsin State Fair, which is famous for its cream puffs.

While hinted at in these interviews, other respondents made more direct links between the fair's celebration of food and the sense of license for excessive and "unhealthy" eating that it promoted; at the same time, many of these visitors contextualized such indulgences as a temporary suspension of their otherwise "sensible" eating practices. Tom, a physician who had already enjoyed a foot-long corn dog and was wrestling with a double-dip waffle ice-cream cone, said that this was "very different" from his regular eating practices but that "all bets are off at the fair." Tom's comment resonates with the observation that "many foods hawked by festival concessionaires succeed commercially, in part, because they lie outside most fans' repertoires of daily dishes or are familiar goods given a new or exotic name" (Adler 1988, 198). Mike and Stephanie, who were at the fair with their children, acknowledged that their lunch, which consisted of barbecued turkey legs, roasted corn, pulled pork sandwiches, and giant pickles, was atypical and predicted that they would be at the EMT station in an hour. Chloe and Jack, an older couple who were sharing an apple dumpling à la mode, said that they eat "much healthier" at home but that once a year it was "okay to splurge." George and Joanne, who were from Palm Springs, California, and who had embarked on a twelve-state tour of state fairs to conduct their own comparative food study, admitted that fair food "is greasier and tastes better," and that while they never eat this way at home, "it doesn't count when you're at the fair."

Ultimately, what these interviews reveal is a simultaneous resistance to and incorporation of culinary capital as demonstrated by the complicated attitudes that fairgoers have about their culinary choices. While some fairgoers seemed earnest about embracing "junk" food as a temporary escape from the social pressure to maintain a "healthy" diet, none of them were particularly earnest in celebrating it as truly good food that they would choose to eat on a regular basis. In fact, most interviewees reacted initially with expressions of guilt as we inquired about their eating practices at the fair. For many of them, this guilt was assuaged by assuming an ironic stance toward what they were eating in an effort to negotiate between competing discourses of excess and restraint. They enjoyed their corn dogs, elephant ears, or deep-fried Twinkies with a wink and a nod, relying upon the contrast between their "normal" lives, in which they supposedly adhered more consistently to healthy eating practices, and their excessive eating at the fair, to mitigate the guilt or feeling of transgression that might otherwise accompany their overindulgence.

Irony allows fairgoers to leverage the culinary capital that they acquire through their regular eating practices, which they characterize as falling in line with the privileged discourses of health and moderation, even as they revel temporarily in the culinary excess invited by the fair. Such a deployment of irony relies upon its "self-protecting function" by "always offering a proviso, always containing a kind of conditional stipulation that undermines any firm or fixed stand" (Hutcheon 1995, 48). In this case, irony provided fairgoers with a way to talk about their food choices without attributing to them any broader meaning or significance. Irony provided the ambiguity and flexibility that allowed fairgoers to negotiate their conflicted desires to identify as good citizens whose daily food practices adhere to calls for healthy and restrained eating and to enjoy their escape from these very mandates. However, rather than threatening their status as culinarily capitalized, such a temporary escape from the privileged eating practices through which culinary capital is typically conferred actually functions to reinforce the value of those practices across the cultural landscape.

As they contrasted their food choices at the fair and in their everyday lives, our interviewees also confirmed a link between culinary capital and a hierarchy that privileges certain foods and food practices over others. Insofar as this fair, like most others, invites its visitors to engage in eating practices that provide an escape from the pressure to maintain a healthy and restrained diet, it functions as a site of resistance against such mandates. Typically, such resistance involves forgoing "healthy" foods that are ascribed to an idealized "high-class" diet, in favor of "unhealthy" food choices that are assigned to the ranks of "low-class" eaters. Such a class-based logic was both confirmed and disrupted by many interviewees who noted that the food at the fair was much more expensive than they had anticipated. Consumers had clearly linked unhealthy eating with inexpensive eating and were surprised to find prices that contradicted their assumptions. Several interviewees indicated that they would have eaten much more if it hadn't been so expensive. Viewed from a broader perspective, the issue of cost reveals the extent to which these unhealthy eating practices, supposedly condemned by mainstream American society, are, in fact, an important source of income not only for the vendors whose livelihood depends upon them, but also the food industry that supplies them and, in the case of state fairs and carnivals, the states, cities, and local municipalities that profit from them.

In fact, while government often regulates food practices—see our discussion below of legal mandates requiring fast food chains to post nutritional information about their products or proposed laws designed to prevent restaurants from serving overweight customers—in this context, states profit from the unhealthy eating practices that are promoted at these fairs and carnivals. Our review of vendor and food concession application templates for various 2010 state fairs reveals that rather than seeking to curtail such presumably "dangerous" behavior, states invite applications from potential food vendors without providing any nutritional guidelines or requiring any information about the health benefits or risks of their proposed menus.[2] While all states in our sample emphasize health and safety in food handling—California, for example, requires applicants to submit a Food Handlers Certificate and actually charges vendors a "Safe Food Handling Fee" that ranges from $110 to $247 per location—we could not find one application that required nutritional information about applicants' proposed menus. The Great New York State Fair, itself no stranger to the monotony of greasy "junk" vendors, notes that it judges vendor applications on "quality, diversity and demand" but provides no further information about what constitutes quality or diversity. The Minnesota State Fair fails to regulate the "healthiness" of its food concessions beyond their adherence to food safety and handling regulations, but its marketing and public relations form for vendors specifically asks food concessionaires if they sell any vegan or gluten-free products, thereby indicating that such an endeavor would be newsworthy. Most states did require a list of menu items, with some states also asking for the proposed price for each item.

Beyond this common component on various applications, we found one condition that would lead a state to impose a restriction of the food products that a vendor could offer, namely an exclusive contract between the state and a specific food or beverage company. For example, the California application includes a section titled "Exclusive Beverage Facility," which reads: "All vendors participating in the State Fair are required to sell Coca-Cola beverages only. Sacramento Coca-Cola Bottling Company will resale product as well as ice. All fountain soda machines, cups, ice merchandisers and related beverages must show the Coca-Cola logo or no logo. Any competing brand signage will not be allowed." Thus, California's only gesture toward regulating what products may be sold and how those products may be displayed comes not from its concern for the health of its citizens but, rather, from the added profitability of an exclusive contract with the Coca-Cola Company. While income to the state coffers may not be the only reason why states seem uninterested in policing the foods and beverages that are sold at their fairs and carnivals, it certainly contributes to an environment that is relatively free from state regulation and that is instead well suited to the government of the self.

To the extent that state fairs promote food choices and practices that contradict those privileged practices that promise culinary capital to consumers who adhere to them, they may be read as promoting an atmosphere of "carnivalesque freedom" marked by "a temporary suspension of...certain norms and prohibitions of usual life" (Bakhtin 1984, 15). However, Bakhtin's emphasis on the temporary nature of this liberation is crucial and was well understood by the fairgoers we interviewed. Echoing Bakhtin's assertion that this carnivalesque freedom exists only as long as the carnival lasts, those who celebrated the excess and pleasure of their state fair dining experiences did so fully aware of the fact that it was a momentary transgression of their normative culinary boundaries. Ironically, this temporary liberation from the demand for healthy and restrained eating can be read as reinscribing the very criteria for culinary capital that it seems to challenge as consumers situate it as an exception to their usual eating practices.

Additionally, to the extent that this transgression occurs within a socially sanctioned space, it is open to a critique that is often waged at Bakhtin's understanding of the carnivalesque, namely that it is "a *licensed* affair in every sense, a permissible rupture of hegemony, a contained popular blow-off as disturbing and relatively ineffectual as a revolutionary work of art" (Eagleton cited in Stallybrass and White 1986, 13). Such public rituals sponsored by the state can be seen as affording elites an occasion to reiterate the moral basis of their authority, defusing possible disruptions by the citizenry by distracting them with revelry (Beezley, Martin, and French 1994, xiii). When applied to state fairs and carnivals, this theory provides another perspective for approaching the question of why states do not actively regulate the types of food and beverages that are available at these events. If this temporary escape serves in the long run to reinforce dietary restraint in the daily lives of the citizenry, then we might conclude that such an escape ultimately strengthens rather than weakens the authority of the state. People are more likely to buy into the project of self-policing if there is at least a brief respite in view, much as we endure calendars consumed with paid labor as long as the week-end is on the horizon.

While such an argument threatens to undermine the radical potential of the carnivalesque in general, and the value of culinary capital in promoting resistance to privileged food practices in particular, Peter Stallybrass and Allon White (1986) provide a framework for valuing such disruptions while acknowledging both their potential and their limitations. Arguing that to posit carnivals as inherently either radical or conservative misses the point, they conclude that "the most that can be said in the abstract is that for long periods carnival may be a stable and cyclical ritual with no noticeable politically transformative effects but that, given the presence of sharpened political antagonism, it may often act as *catalyst* and *site of actual and symbolic struggle*" (Stallybrass and White 1986, 14). Pushing further, they advocate recognizing the carnivalesque as what Roberto da Matta labels "a *privileged locus* of inversion" and emphasize Terry Eagleton's desire to salvage it as a "temporary retextualizing of the social formation that exposes its 'fictive' foundations" (cited in Stallybrass and White 1986, 18). Indeed, individual choices and behaviors that transgress the limits established by the broader social field can, over time, extend those limits and reimagine these fields. As Pauline Adema notes in her study of food festivals, they are "part of a dialectic between structure and agency, may exhibit symbolic reversal of hegemonic social and power relations, express identity, are liminal so potentially transformational, are potentially counter-hegemonic, and may affirm the existing social order" (2009, 36). In other words, it is possible to read fair fare as producing multiple and contradictory forms of culinary capital that promote compliance and resistance simultaneously.

This reading of fairs as contested sites at which culinary capital is utilized to reward both adherence to and resistance of privileged attitudes about food and food practices was literalized at the Indiana State Fair by the contrasting images of food stands selling their deep-fried wares only a few feet away from dieticians and nutritionists promoting Indiana Governor Mitch Daniels's IN-Shape Indiana program. Making the case that "Hoosiers and the companies that employ them have much to gain from improved health," the website of this state Department of Health initiative promotes the centrality of healthy diet and exercise to both individual health and the economic health of the state. INShape Indiana provides an organizing logic for personal and organizational health and fitness initiatives that stand to benefit Hoosiers (residents of Indiana). It offers free consultation with staff nutritionists and personal trainers; generic exercise plans boosted by zingy newsletters and videos that promise "tips for walking!"; directories of fitness events around the state; guidelines for organizing competitive community diets; and an annual Employee Health and Wellness Summit. The program seems motivated primarily by the bottom line, as the idea that "healthy people perform better and save money for themselves, their employers and the state" features prominently on the FAQ page of its website. While it includes a broad range of events and activities across the state, its presence at the state fair is particularly interesting as it exposes the contrasting impulses toward eating—and the conflicting engagements with culinary capital that they signal—that are evident at the fair and that permeate American culture, more broadly.[3]

The side-by-side existence of exhortations to excess evident in the foodstuffs offered by commercial vendors and resolutions of restraint promoted by the INShape campaign provide what Adema describes as a "festival frame" that shapes the expectations of participants and observers. "Within the festival frame...there is license to abandon normative food-related behavior, thus allowing for enjoyment of exotic or unhealthy foods...excessive consumption, and spectaclized eating and cooking through contests" (Adema 2009, 34). Rather than witnessing a clear conflict between those consumers who indulged in the excessive and unhealthy eating promoted at the fair and the INShape representatives who attempted to lure them away from the food stands toward exercise machines and fitness demonstrations, we were struck by the similarities between the comments of the fairgoers and the INShape workers whom we interviewed.

Echoing consumers' attitudes that their ventures into state fair foods were acceptable because they were momentary and exceptional to their "normal" eating practices, the health workers offered similar arguments. Brenda Richardson, past president of the Indiana Dietetic Association, made the point in an interview that "it is fine for someone to say that they are going to have a treat as long as they don't do it every day." She even acknowledged that "funnel cake once a year is okay!" She explained that the governor's central message when it came to a healthy diet was that "it's all about balance" and that the goal of the INShape program was to help people achieve such balance. In short, she offered many of the same platitudes about healthy lifestyles and justifications for the excessive eating taking place at the fair that we had heard from fairgoers themselves, providing another perspective on the flexibility of culinary capital insofar as it was utilized to promote long-term adherence to privileged food practices while adapting to the need for a temporary escape from them.

Ironically, this exposes both the extent to which fairgoers, and arguably the consuming public more broadly, had internalized such attitudes and assumptions about food and the necessity to continually reaffirm them in the face of the competing desire to resist the privileged practices that permeate the contemporary American foodscape. In other words, while indulging in the chocolate-covered bacon, foot-long corn dogs, and deep-fried desserts that are celebrated at the state fair may not translate into a culinary revolution, its potential impact on the American diet is evidenced by the government-sponsored effort to contain such excesses within the temporarily sanctioned space of the state fair. Thus, as fairgoers negotiate the competing calls of the deep-fried food vendors and the INShape dieticians and nutritionists, they underscore the extent to which such sites both reinscribe the attitudes and assumptions about food that dominate contemporary American culture even as they reveal the "fictive foundations" of the current food scene and expose the role of culinary capital in shaping it.

As we saw in our interviews, people take a certain kind of sheepish pride in their edible encounters with the more "junky" and extreme foods at the fair: they know that to be the kind of person who can let his/her hair down enough to indulge in chocolate-covered bacon or fried dough is somehow a good thing, as it signals a flexibility and a lack of uptightness around food. There is status and power in being perceived as that kind of a person in the context of a great deal of anxiety around what we eat. But they also know that such status for the elephant ear–eater is fleeting: to make fair-type food the mainstay of one's diet is to risk a speedy social descent. It is not merely the escape from privileged foodways that is rewarded with status: it is the eternal *return* to them. The true rewards of status accrue to those who identify and frame their fair eating only within the context of their usual food practices, which conform to privileged discourses of health and restraint.

In this way, the space of the fair has fused "the positive emotions of symbols and events with social and moral demands on the subject" (Beezley, Martin, and French 1994, xv) to inculcate subjects who demonstrate culinary capital by trumpeting the virtues of temporary indulgence and its obvious counterpart, long-term restraint. We are especially interested in how the trumpeting of the virtues of restrained, moderate, and healthy eating of food that is fresh, local, and sustainably produced, rather than necessarily the actual *practice* of such foodways, takes ideological priority. Certainly, everyday American food practices are loaded with excess and immoderate consumption of industrially produced foods jetted in from the other side of the globe, so one could almost imagine the food orthodoxies of the upper middle class today as themselves resistant to dominant food practices. In some senses, they are; these food orthodoxies exert a moral pressure with class-based overtones to eat the "right" way, but that is unparalleled by those who engage in more typical American food practices. It is necessary to examine what is at stake for fairgoers and others we examine later in this chapter in their attempts to escape from the pressures to conform to a specific "ascetic aesthetic" of food despite an unrestrained national diet.

While state fairs and carnivals seem to offer only temporary escape from the food orthodoxies of contemporary American culture and, in doing so, may be read as functioning to reinforce the very culinary norms that they challenge, we turn next to other "sites of resistance" that provide a more sustained critique of these orthodox foodways. These sites function less as momentary exceptions to an otherwise conventional routine—the two weeks out of the year during which state fairs and carnivals sanction excessive and unhealthy eating, for example—and more like established countercultural spaces that promote a more consistent challenge to the privileged ideologies that inform the contemporary American foodscape.

Specifically, we read the growing popularity of competitive eating and the emergence of websites dedicated to celebrating "junk" food both as indicators of the intensification of culinary capital across contemporary American culture and as evidence of significant resistance to its usual values hierarchy. These sites, we argue, embrace familiar tropes and utilize modern technology as they promote eating practices that are deemed aberrant and dangerous by those invested in discourses of health and dietary restraint while also framing their criticisms in patriotic and moral terms. While these criticisms can be read as indicators of the extent to which these sites succeed in resisting privileged gastronomic orthodoxies and challenging the broader ideologies that they promote, for instance the racialized fetishization of food production in a romanticized "white farm imaginary" as explored by McCullen (2011), they are not beyond reproach. Instead, we must consider how these sites buy into corporate/industrial food perspectives while relying on publicists and corporate sponsorships for their continued growth. Even with these complications, however, we conclude that these sites do serve not only to contest the dominant culture but ultimately to effect change in the criteria for culinary capital. They do this by embracing excess and pleasure in the eating practices that they celebrate and reframing the terms through which culinary capital is attained.

HEROIC RESISTANCE: THE WORLD OF COMPETITIVE EATING

On July 4, 2009, Joey Chestnut won Nathan's Famous International Eating Contest by eating sixty-eight hot dogs and buns in ten minutes. His victory over the other nineteen competitors, including his archrival, Takeru Kobayashi, who came in a close second with sixty-four-and-a-half hot dogs and buns, was celebrated by a crowd estimated at 40,000 that had gathered on the corner of Surf and Stillwell avenues in Coney Island. For fans who could not be at the event, it was carried live on ESPN. With American flags flying, this patriotic crowd cheered on their hero, who secured America's dominance over its Japanese rival and ensured that the coveted Mustard Belt would remain safely and securely within its borders.

While the Nathan's Hot Dog Eating Contest happens only once a year, it is by no means an anomaly; rather, it is the climax of a year-long cycle of contests sanctioned by the International Federation of Competitive Eating (IFOCE), an organization whose fanatical yet tongue-in-cheek embrace of this "sport" is evidenced by the highly exaggerated assertions and over-the-top tone found on its website. Identifying the Nathan's contest as "the dominant event of the year...which has stood as the de facto Olympics of the sport and as a litmus test of patriotism for eaters of all nations," the IFOCE website's grand claims for this particular event are matched only by its hyperbole-laden history of competitive eating, which it identifies as "among the most diverse, dynamic and demanding sports in history [that] dates back to the earliest days of mankind and stands alongside original athletic pursuits such as running, jumping and throwing." While the IFOCE's exaggerated claims and the cheeky tone with which they are made might cast doubt on the value of a serious analysis of this particular activity, we find that they invite, rather than deter, a consideration of the multiple and nuanced meanings that competitive eating produces. Adrienne Rose Johnson notes, for instance, that the bombastic language of IFOCE announcers "does not simply mock the upper classes but uses its themes to dialectically situate competitive eaters within and against the established traditions of officialdom" (2012, 285). We are particularly interested in how competitive eating rejects adherence to privileged food practices as a means of attaining culinary capital, while simultaneously promoting its own form of culinary capital and utilizing the dual frameworks of patriotism and sport to respond to its detractors and establish its own legitimacy.

In his study of competitive eating, Ryan Nerz traces the rise of competitive eating as a popular/populist phenomenon in contemporary American culture, following its roots back to the state fairs and carnivals that we discussed in the preceding section. He explains that "by the beginning of the twentieth century, pie-eating contests had become as commonplace at fairs and carnivals as tugs-of-war, three-legged races, dunking tanks, judging livestock, potato-sack races, and the beloved challenge of climbing a greased pole" (Nerz 2006, 56). While Nerz explains that these early contests were much more about fun than real competition, he also links them to American national identity and patriotism, particularly during the two world wars.

During World War I, regiments threw pie-eating contests to maintain morale and revel momentarily in their American-ness. As documented in the newspaper *Stars and Stripes,* these contests were held in bold defiance of the act of June 3, 1916, that said "Enlisted men, army bands and members thereof are forbidden from engaging in any competitive civilian employment." The contests resumed during World War II. A captivating photo in the Library of Congress shows a mountainside pie-eating contest held on July 4, 1945, by the Eighty-seventh Regiment of the Tenth Mountain Division in Caporetto, Italy. (Nerz 2006, 56–57)

The theme of patriotic fun continues to inform visitors to the Nathan's Hot Dog Eating Contest.[4] When we asked at the 2009 event why they were drawn to it, many people responded with "It's just fun" and "It's for fun"; members of the ESPN crew who were covering the event recognized that part of its popularity was because spectators found it to be entertaining. Additionally, several spectators gave an overtly patriotic spin to their answers, saying that it was "a great place for family on the 4th of July" and that it was "the perfect 4th of July event—so American!" July 4, which is the anniversary of American independence from Great Britain in 1776, is a federal holiday marked by fireworks, parades, barbecues, picnics, and other festivities celebrating U.S. history, government, and traditions. Hot dogs are consumed at many of these events, as well as at a host of popular sporting events including the U.S. "national pastime," baseball games, so hot dogs are often considered quintessentially American, despite their German origins. For one spectator, the patriotic theme was connected not only to the international competition, but also to the food itself, describing the event "as American as it gets" and the hot dog as "the epitome of American food."

These interviews with fans revealed interesting similarities between their mindsets and those of state fairgoers, which were also echoed in the perspectives shared by competitive eaters. For example, at a clam eating contest held at Peter's Clam Bar on Long Island on Memorial Day 2009, we asked competitors about their participation in eating contests.[5] Most of them made a clear distinction between it and their daily eating habits; for example, Micah Collins (aka Wing Kong) said that he was not a big eater away from competitions. One retired competitor, Ed "Cookie" Jarvis, was enveloped in a long overcoat embroidered with a list of his many victories, and explained that since retiring, he had begun to diet and had already lost a great deal of weight. For these competitors, excessive eating is not a daily habit but, rather, a momentary escape from familiar and generally unquestioned commitments to more restricted dietary practices. Some competitors were amused by people who assumed that because they participated in competitive eating, they ate with reckless abandon on a daily basis. Russ Keeler explained that very often people who know that he is a competitive eater expect him to order extreme amounts of food whenever he goes to a restaurant. He said that his coworkers were surprised when tests conducted at his workplace as part of a wellness program revealed that, despite being a "big guy" and a competitive eater, he was one of the healthiest employees at the company. While his friends and coworkers had assumed that his competitive eating and his larger-than-average body size necessarily translated into bad health, he was pleased that his test results debunked these assumptions.

Like the visitors to state fairs, spectators at this and other competitions also defended competitive eating against charges that it is unhealthy by situating it as a temporary reprieve from a more regulated lifestyle. For example, when asked how he would respond to claims that competitive eating is unhealthy or excessive, one spectator at the Nathan's Hot Dog Eating Contest responded that "one day of gorging is okay." A group of women at the same event explained that while it was "a little over the top," it was just one day of indulgence and that we have to "splurge a little." In this way, spectator and participant narratives at competitive eating events echo those of fairgoers who highlight the temporary nature of their escape from privileged foodways.

Although such sentiments seem initially to limit the long-term impact of competitive eating upon the broader culinary landscape, they do not capture fully the social context or ideological implications of this trend vis-à-vis culinary capital. When read against the culinary orthodoxies that trickle down from upper-middle-class American culture, competitive eating functions as a complex and ambiguous site of resistance to the usual paths to culinary capital. While it may be the case that individual contests, like state fairs, offer only temporary escape from the pressure for dietary restraint and may also function to reinforce prevailing attitudes about health and moderation among competitors and fans alike, we argue that the broader popularity of competitive eating as a countercultural phenomenon functions as a sustained counterbalance to more privileged upper-middle-class culinary practices and trends. As a cultural site these eating contests appear more potentially disruptive of privileged food ideologies than the temporary, state-sanctioned reprieve of the fair as fans and participants resist one set of criteria for attaining culinary capital and formulate a set of standards by which their own claim to it can be adjudicated. In other words, they seek not the revolutionary obliteration of culinary capital and of the power and status that comes with it, but rather a different route to the same destination of power and status.

However, their efforts at doing so do not go uncontested as evidenced in part by the long-standing debate over whether competitive eating should be marginalized as a fringe activity or celebrated as a legitimate sport. Scholar Lawrence Rubin notes that it is tempting to read competitive eaters "as actors in a socially sanctioned gorge fest which represents the 'expression of the social body to establish equilibrium [and] to break free of restraints'" (2008, 253), yet his preferred interpretation runs in a different direction. He argues that competitive eating "represents the fruits of the democratization of professional competitive sport" (Rubin 2008, 253). At the same time that participants and spectators situate competitive eating as a lighthearted escape from their everyday lives, they also frame it around discourses that link it to more mainstream traditional values and ideologies of patriotism and victory, as sports tend to do (Woods 2007). In doing so, they establish familiar criteria through which honor—including the status and power that accompany culinary capital—is to be awarded: namely, by winning. As in all competitive sports, to the victors go the spoils, whether their victory comes from scoring the most points or eating the most hot dogs. In both cases, the designation of "sport" confirms the value of the particular activity and in the specific case of competitive eating, establishes the legitimacy of food practices that run counter to those espoused by privileged voices across the culinary landscape.

From this perspective, we can better understand the pushback against efforts by proponents of competitive eating to define it as a sport with its own rich history and traditions. When baseball manager Lou Piniella dismissed Takeru Kobayashi's ability to eat fifty hot dogs in ten minutes by saying, "That's not a sport.... That's stupidity" (Piniella quoted in Nerz 2006, 141), Rick Shea, cofounder of the IFOCE, responded by suggesting that the comment reveals an economically based territorialism: "Lou Piniella is trying to protect a sport that drives dollars into his pocket... He wants to protect his sport, baseball, because he's threatened by our sport" (Shea quoted in Nerz 2006, 141). Ultimately, Shea argues, those who challenge the legitimacy of competitive eating reveal "a parochial and elitist attitude in sports" (Shea quoted in Nerz 2006, 141). In response, Shea and other defenders of competitive eating make their own cases for identifying competitive eating as a legitimate sport.

Echoing the IFOCE website's exaggerated claim that competitive eating "dates back to the earliest days of mankind," one competitor, "Crazy Legs" Conti, likened it to Roman times in its unique blending of excess and sport when we interviewed him. This sentiment was shared by spectators at the Nathan's Hot Dog Eating Contest. For example, a six-year veteran spectator of this particular contest could cite statistics and records for several competitors and was especially fascinated by the "little guys" and "skinny girls," asking "How do they do it?" and exclaiming, "It's amazing to watch." Another fan defended competitive eating from criticism by explaining that it must be seen as competition, that competitors train for it like a sport and that the Nathan's contest, in particular, was "the Super Bowl of competitive eating." For one group of fans, there was little distinction between this spectacle and that of other major sporting events; they concluded, "It's way less excessive than football." Even spectators who were unsure about its status as a sport acknowledged that the competitors took it very seriously.

A somewhat more playful identification of competitive eating with sports also frames Philadelphia's annual chicken wing eating contest, "Wing Bowl," which began as a publicity stunt conceived of by sports radio personalities Al Morganti and Angelo Cataldi at the *WIP Morning Show*. In tracing Wing Bowl's history, Nerz emphasizes its link to the Super Bowl: "In the early nineties, as the Super Bowl approached each January, Philadelphia Eagles fans found themselves left out. To simultaneously lift the community spirit and mock the Buffalo Bills fans who kept cheering their team to annual Super Bowl losses, the *WIP* crew decided to do what they do best—mock them. Stealing Buffalo's signature foodstuff, the buffalo wing, and borrowing heavily from professional wrestling, they created a cultural event that, while undeniably American, defies explanation" (Nerz 2006, 5–6). While the first Wing Bowl was held in the lobby of a local hotel and attracted 150 spectators, it has since moved to increasingly larger venues as the crowds have grown, settling for the last few years at the Wachovia Center, home of Philadelphia's basketball team, the 76ers. The creators and organizers of Wing Bowl acknowledge that it has evolved into a spectacle where 20,000 fans begin filling the venue at 5:30 A.M., many of whom have been drinking for several hours and are just as attracted to the sexy "wingettes"—young women who have been hand-selected by Angelo Cataldi and his radio show crew to parade around the event in very tight and revealing costumes and to stoke the almost all-male audience into a frenzy—as they are to the competition.

Nonetheless, an event that could easily be identified with the notion of "carnivalesque freedom" that we discussed above does maintain an important, if ambiguous and satirical, link to themes and motifs of sport. Wing Bowl does clearly embrace many familiar elements of the most popular and revered sporting events: Fans don T-shirts of their favorite sports teams; there are extensive statistics, records, and play-by-play commentary; the obligatory national anthem plays at the start of the competition as the Wing Bowl banner hangs high in the rafters honoring past champions and inductees into the Wing Bowl Hall of Fame; the half-time show, which at Wing Bowl 18 featured a rock band and a mechanical bull ridden first by *Jersey Shore* "celebrity" Snooki, aims to entertain; and the event is preceded by the kind of tailgating that happens at many sporting events. But all this happens in a way that exposes the decadence and excess not only of this event, but, arguably, that can be found at the margins of all sports. In doing so, it can be read as embracing excess as a positive attribute rather than demonizing it as a temptation to be resisted and, consequently, elevating it to an attribute for measuring success and a criterion for awarding culinary capital. In this bizarre world, it is those players who are willing to take the most extreme risks of disavowing normative expectations regarding food who face the greatest rewards.

Like Wing Bowl, the 2009 Nathan's Hot Dog Eating Contest was also infused with symbolism that linked it to other sporting events and emphasized its patriotic value—including cheerleaders and mascots, a large plaque painted on the side of the building that records past champions, countless American flags and red-white-and-blue banners, and the singing of the national anthem. At the same time, the event gestured toward the carnivalesque with atmospheric touches like a little person dressed as Uncle Sam warming up the crowd, an energetic trampoline act, and a death-defying feat performed on a bed of nails. For professional gurgitators and their loyal fans, this was a sporting event that featured real competition between elite athletes; however, other spectators identified it more closely with Coney Island's famous freak shows or the Ringling Bros. and Barnum & Bailey Circus, which was installed for the summer just a few blocks away.

These dueling perspectives were captured succinctly in an interview with ESPN staffers. One person who worked on the graphics for the televised coverage acknowledged ESPN's "tongue-in-cheek" attitude, arguing that its treatment of the event as a "real" sport, complete with stats, graphics, and comparisons with other sports, should be read with deep irony. He suggested that ESPN was offering a "one hour joke" presented as a "real" sport and that, ultimately, it was pure entertainment that relied on both subtle and not-so-subtle sarcasm. At the same time, another ESPN staffer recognized that some viewers, fans, and competitors took this much more seriously. He acknowledged that high-speed, high-volume eating was "difficult to do," that these guys are "the best at it," and that it is a real competition. He distinguished between the perspective voiced by his colleague in graphics and that of the people involved who take it very seriously. He emphasized the fact that competitors train hard and that they are professionals for whom this is "their Super Bowl." As with Wing Bowl, it is difficult to draw a clear line between the earnest belief that competitive eating is a legitimate sport and the satirical attitude of those who see such true believers as a source of comic relief, financial gain, or both. Nonetheless, understanding how competitive eating is framed against the broader backdrop of the real and imagined role of sports within American culture is necessary for unpacking how it both resists the privileged criteria according to which culinary capital is typically conferred and establishes its own benchmarks for doing so.

To those who write off competitive eating as a "fringe activity," Nerz cites its growing popularity, from the arena-packing Wing Bowl to televised coverage of the Nathan's Hot Dog Eating Contest on ESPN. In doing so, he frames this specific debate through the discourses of elitism and populism that informed chapter 4's analysis of restaurant review sites like Chowhound. In fact, anti-elitism emerges as a common theme among defenders of competitive eating against those who criticize the eating practices that it promotes and who deny its ability to circulate culinary capital. Echoing the argument of chowhounds against the class-based elitism of traditional restaurant critics and the foodies who follow them, defenders of competitive eating seek to redefine the terms through which culinary capital circulates, namely, from emphasizing elitism and exclusion to adopting an "everyman" approach that embraces a wide variety of food choices and practices that privilege excess over restraint. In short, debates about the legitimacy and value of competitive eating tie directly to tensions within contemporary American culture about what are and what are not "legitimate" ways for acquiring culinary capital.

In fact, this may explain why many detractors of competitive eating vociferously reject its identification as a sport, in part because it promotes ways of eating that fly in the face of privileged eating practices while promising culinary capital to those who excel at and revel in such activities. Their arguments against viewing competitive eating as a sport also reveal the extent to which the identification between players and fans typical in sports has been exploited to inculcate values and ideologies across the cultural spectrum. Within this framework, critics of competitive eating reject its claim to status as a sport because its competitors engage in activities that promote values or behaviors deemed aberrant or deviant. They argue that since sports have traditionally functioned to promote particular investments of physical activity in the healthy body—a goal echoed by proponents of the privileged food practices that promise the reward of culinary capital—we cannot embrace as a "sport" something that authorizes behavior and produces bodies that fall so far afield from the athletic aesthetic. Given that sports in American culture are idealistically woven into the moral fabric of society, critics of competitive eating argue that it is counterproductive to recognize as a sport an activity that is, in fact, a sign of societal decay.

This specific debate over whether competitive eating is a legitimate sport relates directly to its broader function as a site of resistance to the culinary norms and trends that are privileged in contemporary American culture. In a 2003 blog post, Ralph Nader identified competitive eating as one of four "signs of societal decay" as it elevates gluttony to the level of a competitive sport rather than denigrating it as "one of the seven deadly sins" (2003). Like Nader, many critics and commentators take on a highly moralistic tone in their attacks on competitive eating as they connect it to the "obesity epidemic"—"Doctors are appalled. Americans get fatter by the generation, and obesity is listed as the fastest-growing cause of premature death" (Laurence 2002)—or, like Nader, read it as a "grotesque metaphor for America's consumer society" (Laurence 2002). Predictably, critics like George Blackburn, head of the Harvard Medical School nutrition department, enlist their own version of "negative identification" to denounce competitive eating: "We are really concerned because, medically, this sends exactly the wrong message....This kind of behaviour leads to binge addictions. People die from being too fat. To me, the spectacle is macabre" (quoted in Laurence 2002).

Such critiques of competitive eating can be explained in terms that recognize the body as a site for exercising power. "Governments have long targeted the body as a means of creating 'good citizens' as expressed in the 'healthy mind healthy body' dictum. Sport is seen as a healthy physical activity which promotes a fit active body and thus a fully integrated and participating citizen. Boundaries are blurred between the fit, disciplined body and the active citizen. Bodies are also the target of intervention, for example, through the multiple bodies of governmentality, because of the assumption that 'we are our bodies' (Bourdieu and Wacquant 1992) and that citizen selves can be transformed and recreated through body practices" (Woodward 2009, 4). Yet not everyone accepts the equation that a traditionally fit and sporting body makes for a worthy citizen. While Blackburn fears for the viewers and fans of competitive eating who might find in it license for their own overconsumption, for Ryan Nerz such criticisms exacerbate "America's tendency to equate thinness with moral rectitude" (2006, 145).

Citing historian Peter N. Stearns, Nerz argues that "the visceral 'disgusted' reaction that some might feel in watching an eating contest has as much to do with this culturally ingrained association of free eating with laziness and obesity" (2006, 145). Pointing out that some of the best competitive eaters are, in fact, thin, Nerz castigates reporters and critics who single out larger eaters and make them the "objects of their contempt" (2006, 144). Pushing further, Nerz condemns critics for their "dyed-in-the-wool vision of what an athlete looks like" and asks why "in this era of liposuction and salad-picking, all-protein diet fads and anorexic supermodels, where nearly every American feels insecure about his or her body" we do not "exalt the overweight man, or woman who gorges openly" (2006, 145). In short, Nerz challenges the "hateful tone" (2006, 144) of those who use competitive eaters, like the "obese," as scapegoats for their anxieties about increasing American consumerism and what they perceive to be an alarming decay in American values and morals. "The true scandal of sport in the United States is the way it is used to enchant already powerful bodies with even more authority by demonizing already vulnerable others" (Cole 2008, 67). Legitimizing competitive eating upends the established hierarchy of bodies and reframes the terms on which culinary capital circulates. Rather than serving to reinforce prevailing assumptions about "healthy" and "unhealthy" bodies and the kinds of eating practices that are presumed to create them, an alternative set of rules for awarding culinary capital emerges, rules that are based on principles of excess and indulgence rather than restraint and control.

That identification with competitive eaters can motivate fans to question their own eating practices and challenge the broader culinary trends that inform them is made clear by fans like Tom Sorensen, who says that his first move after watching the Nathan's Hot Dog Eating Contest on ESPN was "to put a hot dog on the grill" (2009). Rather than fearing such identifications as leading to the downfall of American society, Sorensen celebrates them, suggesting that his own diet, which includes "pouring low-fat milk on my cereal and no-fat milk into my latte," "eat[ing] red meat at most twice a week," and "rarely eat[ing] desserts," has taken him astray from his own forefathers, who "killed dinosaurs and buffalo" (2009).[6] As Sorensen invites his readers to "enjoy Coney Island's consuming carnivores" (2009), he gets to the heart of the role that competitive eating can play in resisting privileged attitudes and assumptions that typically determine one's access to culinary capital and championing an alternative set of criteria for such access. Like state fairs and carnivals, competitive eating contests invite consumers to engage in eating practices that may be dismissed as "low-class"—code for excessive and unhealthy—and to challenge those who base their claim to culinary capital on adherence to a set of privileged dietary norms and practices that they believe should dominate the contemporary American food scene.

However, while the impact of any individual eating contest is limited, even if it packs an arena with 20,000 fans or is carried live on ESPN, the increased visibility and celebration of competitive eating across the cultural landscape suggests a more sustained and potentially effective form of resistance to those privileged foodways. With an increase in the number of television shows that celebrate competitive and excessive eating, including the Travel Channel's reality show *Man v. Food* and its series dedicated to "extreme" eating, it is difficult to argue that the influence of competitive eating has been contained. While the state fair ends and the carnival closes, the celebration of extreme eating continues, and we may arrive at the point where those who preach health and dietary restraint find themselves confronted by a consuming public that challenges their authority to define the terms through which culinary capital is conferred and stakes its own claim to culinary capital based on the pleasure of indulgence rather than the benefits of restraint. Sustained resistance, in other words, can lead to more than just a temporary escape from the prevailing privileged practices that promise culinary capital to those who adhere to them; instead, it can motivate a shift in the very criteria through which culinary capital is to be measured and conferred.

While competitive eating does challenge prevailing culinary dogma and, as such, functions as an important site of resistance to a range of contemporary food trends, its meteoric rise has been made possible, to a significant degree, by embracing both the mainstream media and the economic opportunities that come with increased visibility and popularity. This transition from state fair pastime and carnival sideshow to cultural phenomenon complete with "corporate sponsorship, lucrative cash prizes, and a league of semi-professional eaters" (O'Connor 2007) began in the 1990s as public relations gurus George and Rich Shea, who had been working for the men who had invented the Nathan's Hot Dog Eating Contest, took over this account and created the IFOCE "with the goal of extruding that single hot dog contest into a gluttonous empire" (Fagone 2006, 15). They quickly signed top-tiered eaters to exclusive management contracts and lined up corporate sponsorships for their events.

At the same time, they marketed competitive eating very carefully to a specific demographic, the "guy demo" (Fagone 2006, 15). As Rich Shea explains, "People are tired of coddled professional athletes with ridiculous salaries. Gurgitators are regular guys, and while it might be nice to watch superstars like

Derek Jeter compete, it's refreshing to see normal guys excel at something they're good at. Plus, it's no secret that Americans are big eaters, so competitive eating appeals to them. It's the sport of the everyman, and I think people are right when they say it's going to be the next big thing" (Shea quoted in O'Connor 2007). Recognizing Shea's talent for exploiting the "everyman" motif to promote competitive eating, O'Connor reports that IFOCE-sanctioned contests serve as "promotional vehicle[s] for corporate brands" and that "contests themselves can seem almost secondary to the publicity they afford their benefactors" (2007). In addition, while professional gurgitators will never match the earnings of top professional athletes in mainstream sports, contests have become more lucrative. "In 2005, sponsors shelled out more than $150,000 in prize money" and while in the past "eaters rarely received more than a plastic trophy," today "four- and five-figure grand prizes are not uncommon" (O'Connor 2007).

Ryan Nerz's celebration of competitive eating as the sport for "regular Joes" warrants interrogation given the fact that it is an acknowledged public relations strategy aimed at increasing profitability. Yet it is also true that George and Rich Shea's success in popularizing this narrative is due, at least in part, to a culinary landscape that was in need of an alternative to the mantras of health and dietary restraint that permeate American culture. By pitching competitive eating to "every man" and giving its audience license to revel in excess and overindulgence, the Sheas have exposed the elitism of the presumed culinary mainstream and have appropriated their own share of culinary capital. But the symbolic buck does not stop with the slick, ironic Sheas: fans and competitive eaters are also licensed by the spectacle to articulate critiques, however fraught with internal contradiction, of privileged food orthodoxies of restraint, moderation, and quality, thus garnering for themselves on their own terms some share of culinary capital. "The very act of eating to excess and getting one's money's worth for food becomes more important than any affected interest in a chef's culinary skill or training" (Halloran 2004). The emphasis on quantity over quality, the disregard for the "slow" vogue championed by proponents of the international Slow Food movement (Greene 2011), and the agnostic attitude toward culinary pretense voiced by fans and eaters undermine presumably sacrosanct orthodoxies about food, even as they earn those who voice them subcultural status and power.

EATING AND PLEASURE: ONLINE COMMUNITIES OF "JUNK FOODIES"

In *The Junk Food Companion: The Complete Guide to Eating Badly*, humorist Eric Spitznagel laments that "we've allowed ourselves to become victims of nutrition fascism. A tight tummy and unclogged arteries may sound appealing in theory, but when that beast inside our bellies starts calling out for satisfaction, our natural instinct is to eat what *tastes* good over what's good for us every time. It's not just common sense; it's what separates us from the lower animals" (1999, 2). In addition to emphasizing taste, Spitznagel also reminds his readers that "eating is supposed to be fun," concluding that our society's emphasis on health food contradicts this impulse: "As much as we try to deny it, health food will never be as interesting to us as junk food. Health food can only offer sustenance, and sustenance can get pretty boring after a while" (1999, 2). What is lost in this healthy diet, he argues, is pleasure: "You'll never find a prize inside a container of low-fat yogurt, there's no thrill in seeing how many bran muffins you can consume before you pass out, and there isn't a vegetable around that has a lovable cartoon mascot to call its own. Only junk food offers that kind of amusement" (Spitznagel 1999, 3). Tongue planted firmly in cheek and sounding very much like one of the Shea brothers promoting a competitive eating event, Spitznagel exhorts readers: "Continue eating junk food as often as possible and ignore the heretics who would ruin your fun with their contemptible scare tactics" (1999, 212).

While Spitznagel may hyperbolize for the sake of humor, he raises important issues that warrant serious consideration as we explore alternate routes for accessing culinary capital. From a biological perspective, food scientist Steven Witherly provides an evolutionary justification for our enjoyment of "junk" by exploring variables like sensation, caloric load, taste hedonics, emulsion preferences, and salivation responses (2007, 19). Witherly explains the biological principle of "super normal stimulus," which holds that "rare and important stimuli in the environment (like energy-dense foods) become magnified and more desirable (or Super Normal) if made *larger* than expected. . . . Many of our favorite foods are supernormal combinations of salt, fat, and sugar that exceed anything available to our wandering ancestors. We evolved to crave these valuable and rare nutrients. Hence, we respond with an exaggerated eating response (hyperphagia) to the super normal sundae" (2007, 9). A former Food and Drug Administration Commissioner spins the kind of argument that Witherly makes, but with the intent to politicize. David Kessler (2009) contends that such drives for sugar, fat, and sheer volume have been stoked from embers to burning flames by an industrial food system that stands to profit from overconsumption by Americans. Whether comedic, scientific, or political, explanations for the embrace of "junk food" in a culture seemingly obsessed with health, diet, and body size invite further analysis.

In chapters 2 and 4, we examined how the Internet has emerged as an important site for promoting the privileged attitudes and assumptions about food that shape individuals' claims to culinary capital; however, we also want to consider how it also provides a space for resistance as it promotes food practices that undermine these values and, in doing so, establishes an alternative framework for accessing culinary capital. For every website that promotes healthy eating, challenges the industrial food system, or implores Americans to make "wiser" food choices that are "better" for themselves and for the environment, there are as many websites that celebrate indulgence, promote excess, and elevate "junk" food to the status of haute cuisine. Like the restaurant review sites discussed in chapter 4, sites dedicated to "junk" food function to create a community of "junk foodies" who can openly and unapologetically embrace their love of these treats free from recrimination. Such sites, including Junkfoodie.com, Junkfoodblog.com, and Livingonjunkfood.com, promote eating practices radically different from those espoused by nutritionists and any number of very successful contemporary food writers. Even as corporate sponsorships and product advertisements reveal a financial incentive that may complicate their motives, these sites nonetheless create an important alternative space for those seeking to resist the broader social pressure to privilege health and dietary restraint as prerequisites for accessing culinary capital.

While each of these sites strikes a note of resistance as it explains its origins and purpose, some of the sentiments they express suggest varying degrees of resistance by individual consumers, especially those who seem to have bought in to a corporate, heavily marketed "alternative" discourse of what is "good" or "desirable." Nonetheless, the cumulative effect of these sites and the celebration of junk food that they promote warrant serious consideration insofar as they, like the competitive eating contests that we discussed above, establish alternative criteria for conferring culinary capital. For example, on Junkfoodie, site founder Manolito Montala explains, "Despite the campaign about health and nutrition, we can't resist eating or gorging ourselves on junk food. We are always advised to eat health foods like fresh fruits and vegetables and avoid fatty and animal products as much as possible. But because of commercials and attractive packaging and advertising we can't resist to purchase and eat those things. Let's face it—LIFE IS BORING WITHOUT JUNKFOOD!"

Similarly, Steve Johnson, founder of Junk Food Blog, offers this defiant note on his blog as he explains his motivation to create the site: "Tired of eating soy-cheese? Wondering why you starve yourself all morning only to replenish yourself with carrot sticks? Then you need to bookmark Junk Food Blog! Junk Food Blog reports on the newest junk food hitting the market, giving you plenty of options to satisfy your lust for fat, sugar, salt, and alcohol (you know, the stuff you *really* want). We celebrate the stuff we Americans were meant to eat, the stuff we became famous for. . . . Drop the turkey-breast sandwiches and tofuberry shakes. Go get the Pringles, the Little Smokies, the Krispy-Kremes, the Ben & Jerry's! It's ok. Just tell yourself, it's ok. Bookmark Junk Food Blog, and do the American thing."

Doug, founder of Livingonjunkfood, offers the following observations in his initial post: "In today's world, everyone says that they are eating healthier, shopping for organic fruits & vegetables, free range meat & chicken, wild caught fish, and whole grain bread. BUT.... Let's face it, despite all these claims, there's a dark side of eating that people just don't talk about. It happens in your car, on the way home from a tough day at work...your car almost drives itself thru the drive-thru.... It happens late at night, after everyone has gone to bed. You sneak down to the kitchen, and reach into the cupboard above the spice rack...hidden way in the back is that bag of Oreo Cookies.... Or buried in the back of the freezer behind the '100% Fruit Juice Pops' is that carton of Ben & Jerry's 'Phish Food'...Yes, Junk Food is the dirty secret that everyone hides & doesn't talk about."

These populist manifestos share some common themes. First, they each emphasize resisting certain contemporary food trends, including campaigns about health and nutrition that amount to severely restricting diets and fetishizing organic and natural foods. Additionally, they link such trends to living lives that are thought to be, like the diets they promote, unsatisfying and boring. Like Eric Spitznagel, they remind us of our desire to eat things that taste rich and leave us feeling satisfied. While predominant voices within the contemporary food movement suggest that a healthy diet and a pleasurable eating experience are not necessarily mutually exclusive, the founders of these websites are not buying this argument. For them, the mandate to eat healthy is, inevitably, a call to deny oneself the pleasure of eating food that really tastes good. Johnson's patriotic theme is especially interesting. Like the IFOCE in its framing of competitive eating, in general, and the Nathan's Hot Dog Eating Contest, in particular, Johnson positions his community of "junk foodies" not outside of the mainstream but, rather, as doing "the American thing," by celebrating "the stuff we Americans were meant to eat." American revolutionaries are thus reimagined as those daring individualists who refuse, like their forebears, to submit to the rules of the powers that be. The king of England, in this mindset, has been replaced by Michael Pollan, but requires every bit as much resistance.

In each instance, eating junk food is linked to embracing what they identify as a basic human need, echoing Steven Witherly's evolutionary theory, while also linking it to the fulfillment of other desires. As Johnson offers his site as providing his readers plenty of opportunities to satisfy their "lust" and Doug catches us succumbing to the "dark side" of eating, whether by sneaking through a fast food drive thru window or tiptoeing into the kitchen late at night for that forbidden snack, these culinary desires are sexualized and the mandate to resist them takes on familiar moral and religious undertones.[7] Like Ralph Nader's critique of competitive eating as a sign of society's moral decay, those who condemn the guilty pleasures associated with junk food do so by connecting it to a range of other taboo tastes and desires (see Nutter 2008 for more on this phenomenon).

In the face of such criticism, these and similar websites share the desire to create communities of junk foodies who can celebrate junk food free of criticism and condemnation. We contend that as they do so, they also establish within these alternative communities their own rules for acquiring culinary capital that typically defy privileged food practices and the values they portend to promote. In this formulation, the most extreme affection for junk garners the largest reward of subcultural status. Bloggers pursue this status as they post information, news, and reviews about all things junk food related, provide a forum for discussion, and validate tastes, pleasures, and food practices that are otherwise discounted as outside of the idealized mainstream. For example, Junkfoodie organizes its posts into several categories, including cookies, cakes, candies, chips, chocolate, and snacks. Some of the more popular categories on Junk Food Blog are brownies, cakes, candy, candy bars, chocolate, cookies, doughnuts, fast food, ice cream, and meat snacks. Most posts begin with information about and reviews of new or updated food products and are often followed by comments from readers. Sometimes these comments provide additional information or ask questions; other times, they spark lively debate. A post on Junk Food Blog, for instance, highlights a recent announcement by McDonald's that its breakfast sandwich, the McSkillet Burrito, would soon be available nationwide. This generated lively discussion as bloggers debated this decision. While some celebrated it—one blogger, for example, confesses that while he was never a fan of McDonald's breakfast, now he finds himself "coming up with excuses to go to McDonalds for breakfast and even saying I am not hungry then sneaking off there"—others offered sharp criticism of this new item, including Ken, who after eating one was left wondering if "the cook forgot to add some ingredients," and an anonymous poster who dismissed it as "the worst breakfast item I have ever consumed."

For these bloggers, junk food warrants serious attention, can produce vigorous debate, and can serve as a means for accessing culinary capital within their community. In this way, these sites function in ways that are similar to the popular restaurant review sites that we discussed in chapter 4. Like those sites, these junk food blogs invite participation and operate with an egalitarian impulse but, as we saw on the Chowhound discussion boards, such democratic aspirations are not always put easily into practice. While a significant portion of these blogs is dedicated to presenting information about new products or developments within the junk food industry, discussions boards can generate debate and, consequently, echo the questions about authority within a supposedly free and democratic virtual world (as addressed in chapter 4). Like Chowhound, Junk Food Blog includes updates on and reviews of a variety of fast food and chain restaurants, including Cracker Barrel, Bob Evans, Chili's, Bob's Big Boy, Pizza Hut, and Carl's Jr. Posters usually share a recent dining experience, which often leads other posters to share their own experiences, memories, and opinions.

For example, a post about a menu change at Bob's Big Boy promulgated a lengthy discussion of this restaurant's past, present, and future. After one poster asks what has happened to this restaurant chain, one blogger responds that she will be working at a new Bob's Big Boy set to open in Temecula, California, and another divulges that he had once created a Bob's Big Boy Halloween costume and given its popularity, began making appearances as the unofficial Bob's Big Boy mascot. Many other bloggers recount fond childhood memories of eating at Bob's Big Boy, one of whom offers one complaint following a return visit: "My only complaint is that it's too small, and the booths are made for skinny people. Bob's has to assume that their customers are not a size 2, and their booths should accommodate a bigger person!" This criticism relates to a post from Mike, who responds to another blogger's lament that Bob's menu "does not exactly coincide with a healthy lifestyle" by recalling "memories of times when we didn't care about trans-fats, calories or sodium." Clearly, these restaurant reviews and the discussions they generate demonstrate the extent to which even junk foodies are impacted by the discourses of health, diet, and nutrition that dominate today's culinary scene, even as some bloggers resist such trends or recall a time in which they, and perhaps the broader culture, were less consumed by them. Such nostalgia also serves to acknowledge the arbitrariness and transience of the rules for accessing culinary capital that are privileged at a particular historical moment and to signal the viability of promoting different rules within alternative cultural sites like these junk food communities.

Another way in which junk food websites function to resist privileged culinary trends and attitudes is to provide a space in which they can be challenged, including by responding to specific manifestations of them across the cultural landscape. In seeking to level the culinary playing field, these sites circulate alternative viewpoints and undermine the ability of the culinary elite and their acolytes to stake an exclusive claim to culinary capital. For example, Junk Food Blog includes a section labeled "politics" where bloggers can address a range of food-related issues and debates. In one post, titled "Fast Food for Thought," Steve responds to a *60 Minutes* piece on New York City Health Commissioner Thomas Frieden's effort to require fast food restaurants to include caloric information on their menu boards. *60 Minutes* correspondent Leslie Stahl sets up her story with an all-too-familiar diatribe against obesity rates that are spiraling out of control, citing as a cause for this "epidemic" the fact that so many Americans are now eating out. While food packaging in grocery stores includes dietary information, allowing consumers to make informed choices, Stahl suggests that diners cannot do so when they eat in restaurants that do not divulge this information.

Ostensibly, then, Frieden's effort to require restaurants to post such information on their menus is about providing consumers with information so that they can make informed choices. In his post, Steve points out the ways in which Stahl's piece strays from this initial set-up. First, he argues, the piece never acknowledges the fact that consumers already have a choice not to eat fast food: "Instead, Leslie Stahl made it appear as if Americans *don't* have a choice. Instead of saying that Americans can buy fresh food from the grocery store, she made it appear that we're forced to buy meals from fast-food." In other words, rather than contrasting an uninformed consumer who is duped into eating unhealthy food with an informed consumer who, armed with caloric and other dietary information, would obviously choose not to eat such food, Steve speaks up for the consumer who exercises his or her own agency and chooses to eat fast food. While this choice may be informed by any number of factors, Steve zeros in on the aspect of class that is entirely absent from Stahl's report.

Frieden offers his own explanation for why his law would only require this posting at fast food chains, namely because they already make this information available on their websites so this is just an extension of what they already do, and Stahl never problematizes this formulation. Yet Steve sees the issue rather differently, casting it in class terms: "I guess it's okay if the rich die young." In speculating as to why Frieden's efforts are directed at venues presumed to cater to lower-class eaters, he exposes the fissure in the paternalism of measures that are enacted to protect presumably uneducated and ignorant lower-class consumers who would otherwise eat themselves to death on cheap fast food. Does Frieden focus on these consumers because he assumes that upper-class eaters are better educated and, thus, more likely to make the "right" food choices for themselves or, as Steve sarcastically suggests, does he not care about them? Ultimately, Steve uses his own media outlet to challenge this attack on the fast food industry and its presumably lower-class patrons; in doing so, he exposes the fallacies in these familiar arguments and shifts the terms of the debate in ways that seek to privilege alternative eating practices and to confer culinary capital upon those who choose to engage in them.

A second post included in the politics section of the Junk Food Blog generated one of the site's most vociferous responses. Titled "Mississippi HB 282—Denying Food to Obese," this post concerns a bill introduced in the Mississippi legislature that would make it illegal for restaurants to serve fat people. Steve quotes the bill: "Any food establishment to which this section applies shall not be allowed to serve food to any person who is obese, based on criteria prescribed by the State Department of Health after consultation with the Mississippi Council on Obesity Prevention and Management established under Section 41–101–1 or its successor." This post generated nineteen comments that simultaneously circulate and challenge many of the ideologies that inform contemporary food culture. Some bloggers express concern about the uncritical proliferation of the concept of "obesity": John A. writes, "Note that many professional athletes have BMI of 30 or more." Laura K. notes that, "According to my BMI I'm obese yet I'm very healthy!" Another anonymous poster links anti-fat prejudice to the history of racial discrimination: "This is just more Jim Crow, updated for the 21st Century." Across the range of responses lies a common theme, namely the desire to challenge the policing of individual dietary choice in the name of a broader social well-being. Ultimately, this discussion demonstrates one of the important ways in which this website, and others like it, not only create a community of "junk foodies," but also how they in turn use this network to challenge those who would foist contemporary privileged gastronomic values upon them and, in doing so, demonize the foodways of those lower down the socioeconomic ladder.

What these websites and the world of competitive eating share is a sustained and growing presence that challenges the privileged discourses of health and dietary restraint that permeate the contemporary American food scene where people seem to be more interested in self-denial than the actual consequences of their foodways (Stein 2008, 68). Like fairs and carnivals, they authorize indulgence and pleasure as acceptable criteria for making food choices and for conferring culinary capital; however, rather than doing so in a limited or temporary fashion, they occupy a more sustained alternative space within American culture and, as such, provide an important counterbalance to those voices that seem to dominate the culinary landscape. Fairgoers who sample a full range of deep-fried delectables, competitive eating fans who celebrate the athletic abilities of their favorite gurgitators while putting their own hot dogs on the grill, fast food enthusiasts who swing unapologetically through the drive-thru window, junk food consumers who engage in discussion and debate about their favorite treats with the same energy and enthusiasm that is too often reserved for the "high-end" food scene—all of these eaters participate in acts of culinary resistance.

At the same time, as competitive eaters and their fans garner increased public attention and as "junk foodies" emerge as legitimate sources of revenue for the products that they promote and the businesses that support them, they underscore the fact that culinary capital is not owned by any one segment of society but, rather, that it is continually up for grabs. While we may be witnessing an increase in the ability to access culinary capital by embracing excess and pleasure rather than restraint and self-control, we should also be mindful of the fact that what may at first seem to be a revolution is, in fact, a cyclical return. Certainly, predilections for excess and personal pleasure have gone hand-in-hand with capital before in other times and places (Whitmeyer 1996)—the reigns of Henry VIII in sixteenth-century England, Louis

XVI in eighteenth-century France, Caligula in Rome in the first century A.D., for instance—and not usually for the good of the people. Nonetheless, to the extent that competitive eaters and "junk" foodies establish their own terms and criteria for claiming culinary capital within their admittedly alternative communities, they underscore the very arbitrariness of *which* eating practices earn privilege and bring culinary capital.

Conclusion

The preceding chapters show that culinary capital moves across the land-scape of contemporary American culture in complex ways. As individuals make their own food choices, we witness culinary capital in action as those choices align with or challenge the broader cultural values and ideologies that inform them. We see this as meal assembly kitchens and e-grocers market themselves as solutions for modern women who face the conflict between their own ambitions and the traditional role within their families that they seek to fulfill. We recognize it as the Food Network continually adapts its programming to reflect, and thus reinforce, attitudes and expectations about class and gender that permeate contemporary American society. We find it as online restaurant review sites juxtapose themselves with traditional forms of restaurant criticism as they claim egalitarianism and democracy as their guiding principles only to establish their own hierarchies and embrace their own exclusionary definitions of "authenticity" and "taste." In each of these examples, and in many other social spaces in which food and foodways are negotiated, we see a pursuit of culinary capital that requires adherence to a set of privileged practices, thereby reinforcing specific cultural values and ideologies.

While meal assembly businesses and e-grocers, food television, and res-taurant review websites are all capitalist endeavors motivated by the need to generate profit, they do so by enabling consumers to make food-related choices that are connected to their sense of self. For the consumer, being able to say "I made that 'Healthy Lifestyles Lemon Dill Tilapia' at Dinner By Design for my family because I care about what they eat" speaks to her/his self-identification as someone who will trade money, and a modest amount of time and effort, to engage in caretaking activity that produces a tasty and nutritious meal for the family. Ordering the Tabla Chicken Coconut Curry with Basmati Rice 4-Minute Meal from Fresh Direct is not just refueling, it is also asserting that the orderer is savvy about trendy Manhattan eateries, has a yen for the exotic, and has a life so bursting that cooking has to be fast to fit it all in. Choosing whether to watch and possibly admire and emulate Paula Deen or Robin Miller is also a way of communicating about oneself as a con-sumer: "I value authenticity, and I think good food takes time" or "I'm on the go, and I want to give my family the best on a dime and in a hurry." Even the online restaurant review communities like Chowhound and Yelp, which arguably give participants the most viable opportunities to shape discourse, exist for the very purpose of aggregating knowledge about commercial enterprises; in other words, it is good for business, in the same sense that "there's no such thing as bad publicity." Announcing to the world why you think Jean Georges is better than Per Se allows you to get a little piece of the expertise pie and toot your own horn at the same time: "Look ma! I can afford to eat at super high-end restaurants, multiple times, and I have the good sense and great taste to be able to mete out the finer points of each experience!" The common theme in all of these venues for culinary capital is that people are encouraged to make choices that are in line with a particular narrative about our culture's values and priorities around food. In doing so, they individually and collectively reinforce this very narrative.

However, we have also examined other paths to culinary capital that do not fall in line with this particular narrative but, instead, indicate how it is continually reshaped and potentially rewritten. Visitors to state fairs and carnivals enjoy their corn dogs, elephant ears, and deep-fried candy bars. Fans of competitive eating cheer on their favorite gurgitators, and "junk foodies" take to the Internet to talk about their favorite treats or compare notes on their favorite chain restaurants. In countering privileged foodways, they all stake claims to culinary capital.

Rather than suggesting that the terms through which culinary capital is accessed remain stable, we are most interested in how they are continually renegotiated in ways that respond to and reflect the broader culture at any particular moment. In fact, we conclude that what makes one path to culinary capital any more legitimate than another is completely arbitrary, but those with symbolic capital have the capacity to establish their route to culinary capital as privileged insofar as they are authorized to make their claims about reality stick. In the mainstream U.S. context, that means that educated, upper-middle-class tastemakers—writers and thinkers—are most likely to shape the food orthodoxies of the day. At the same time, rather than dismissing the worlds of competitive eating and the junk food blogosphere as outside of this mainstream, we want to underscore the fact that they serve an important role, namely upending our perspective on what is and what is not a legitimate path to culinary capital.

HYBRID FOODWAYS AND THE NEW CULINARY CAPITAL

While the power and status that come with culinary capital have been appropriated most commonly by those in the mainstream who adhere to and endorse privileged foodways, in subcultural spaces, culinary capital is a reward for those who most daringly subvert those privileged foodways and animate their own set of alternative beliefs and practices. However, rather than setting up an inevitable and intractable binary between exclusively elite, privileged, health-and-restraint dominated foodways, on the one hand, and resistant excess and indulgence, on the other hand, we conclude that the greatest capacity for reward comes from those who meld within their foodways these seemingly contradictory paths to culinary capital. Rather than an empty gesture that harkens back to the concept of omnivorousness that we discussed in chapter 1, we see a growing trend toward such melding as potentially transformative.

Specifically, we want to consider three spaces in which we see this happening: restaurants, supermarkets, and food-related television. In each of these spaces, we are beginning to see privileged food discourse making room for excess and indulgence, as we also witness low-status foodways incorporating a focus on health, restraint, and sustainability, in both cases earning those who inhabit those spaces culinary capital for their food choices and practices. The pursuit of these hybrid foodways by legions of consumer citizens looking for rewarding ways to remake their individual identities stands to transform what constitutes privileged food discourse, disrupting its often Puritanical bent, just as it promises to alter resistant, subcultural food discourse, perhaps undermining its unwitting allegiance to Big Food. In hybrid foodways, we perhaps see the faint contours of the truly democratic food culture called for by Johnston and Baumann (2010, 210)—one that not only privileges good taste and deliciousness but also incorporates environmental and social justice concerns (see also Rousseau 2012).

The result is possibly a saner food space for all of us, one that makes quality, nutritious, sustainably produced food accessible to all those who want it when they want it, and one that allows—even encourages—a more playful, relaxed attitude toward "junkier" food among those who want it, when they want it. While this shift does seem to align with omnivorousness, we see an important difference. While a top-down approach to omnivorousness invites primarily high-end consumers to earn culinary capital by dabbling in the foodways of the Other, the form of hybridization that we discuss here promotes a more complicated interplay between privileged and non-privileged foodways.

Hybrid Restaurants

Such melding is visible in both the higher-end and lower-end of the restaurant spectrum as trendy, upscale eateries market excessive and unhealthy eating practices to their elite clientele and as chain restaurants make healthier food choices accessible to consumers who lack the economic capital that has heretofore been necessary to adopt such practices as part of their everyday diets. While restaurants that emphasize healthy, organic, and/or locally acquired foods continue to populate the culinary scene, other restaurants suggest a shift in the culinary winds. The popular Los Angeles restaurant Animal captures this change as a trendy spot for elite eaters to rack up 3,000 calories per plate of food. Animal epitomizes a contradiction that Dana Goodyear reads as a central feature of Los Angeles's culinary identity: "Faithful to its roots as a tubercular colony, Los Angeles is a city of juice fasts, tonics, and brown-rice cleanses; its image of itself depends on rigorous abstinence from comfort food. But there is a countercurrent of roadside stands, drive-ins, and food trucks, which along with grilled pizza and Cobb salad, arguably constitute the true regional cooking of Southern California" (Goodyear 2010, 34). What makes Animal unique, Goodyear suggests, is that it has taken traditionally marginalized food practices and put them at the center of Los Angeles's cultural and culinary scene, with such positive reception that the lines are often more than three hours long.

However, while Animal is frequented by celebrities and celebrity chefs alike, it is not without criticism. Goodyear (2010, 35) cites a 2008 review by S. Irene Virbila, the restaurant critic for the *L.A. Times*, who "praised Shook and Dotolo's technique but accused them of overkill: too much bacon, too much sauce, too much sugar, too much salt, not enough vegetable." Goodyear quotes Virbila: "What's needed are some perspective and discipline" (2010, 35). This call for "discipline" connects the example of Animal to the tension between "privileged" and "resistant" food practices that informs our broader analysis of culinary capital. At the same time, the popularity of Animal within the trendy Los Angeles food scene suggests that it is more than an exception that can be banished to the culinary and cultural margins—as one may be tempted to do with competitive eating or "junk" food blogs—that it in fact reflects a broader change in the kinds of eating experiences that high-end consumers are seeking and the broader values and attitudes that are shaping their choices.

Another example of melding between privileged and non-privileged food practices is found in Bark Hot Dogs in Park Slope, Brooklyn. Although there is a clear distinction between the industrially produced and non-hygienically prepared "dirty water" dogs available at vending carts across New York City and the "artisanal amalgam of pork and beef" hot dogs, served with a variety of fresh, homemade toppings, available at Bark Hot Dogs, the fact remains that a presumably low-class item like the hot dog finds itself elevated into a viable choice for consumers who want to emphasize health and sustainability through their food choices (Peed 2009). In other words, the menu at Bark Hot Dogs marks an important shift away from celebrating certain foods and food choices as privileged over others as it takes a food item generally assumed to be low class and reinvents it. Such blurring, we argue, signals a shift not only in the kinds of food choices and practices that are privileged, but also in the broader attitudes and assumptions that inform them.

What does it say about the privileged status of contemporary upper-middle-class foodways when those who espouse them and seek to gain status from them flock to Animal, a temple of excess, or to Bark Hot Dogs, to indulge their taste for the lowly wiener? We conclude that as celebrities and celebrity chefs line up outside of Animal to wait for their "gnarly big plates of food" (Goodyear 2010, 34) and as Bark's owners transform the hot dog into a viable choice for trendy foodies, we are witnessing a move away from the privileged food practices that have promised culinary capital to those who adhere to them. In their place, Animal, Bark Hot Dog, and a number of other trendy and upscale restaurants are experimenting with menus that reflect a very different set of tastes and desires, including a celebration of supposedly "low" foods that cannot be characterized as healthy choices for restrained eaters. We read such forays across culinary boundaries as challenging the assumption that specific foods and food practices, in and of themselves, are to be privileged over others.

At the same time that high-end restaurants are experimenting with menus that extend beyond the confines of privileged food practices, we see chain and fast food restaurants expanding their own menus in an attempt to make healthier food choices available to their consumers. Fast food restaurants, usually thought to be the embodiment of indulgent, excessive, and junky food-ways, also show hybrid receptivity to privileged foodways. Few and far between are fast food restaurants that have failed to concede to discourses of health and restraint by offering nutritious options. Wendy's website, for instance, trumpets the fact that its burgers are never frozen, its tomatoes are hand sliced, and its apples are hand picked, in a nod to the current favor for sustainable practices. It also offers suggestions for different meals "that fit your healthy lifestyle" and provides choices including salads and baked potatoes that are (if one holds the dressing) relatively low in calories and fat. Whether the concern for customers' health that is articulated by Wendy's and other fast food chains is genuine is arguable; certainly, they want their customers to live, in order to buy more food. What these restaurants truly emphasize, more than health, is consumer *choice*. "At Wendy's, we believe in choice. Choice in toppings. Choice in dressings. And the choice to select from a wide variety of nutritious options," claims the webpage. The reasons for the hybridization of fast food restaurants are dubious, but not the results: we have witnessed a transformation of the fast food menu in the last twenty years that democratizes the possibility of being rewarded with status for making certain choices from what they offer. The some-time Wendy's slogan "It's waaaaay better than fast food" dramatizes the hierarchy of taste that its upward-reaching offerings target, thus offering customers the capacity for distinction while still eating in the way of the masses.

Grocers and Hybridity

Like restaurants, we are also witnessing interesting shifts in the kinds of food choices that supermarkets are making available to their customers. Wal-Mart, in alliance with First Lady Michelle Obama, announced in January 2011 a five-year plan to reduce the salts, fats, and sugars in the packaged food they sell, and to lower the costs of fruits and vegetables (Stolberg 2011, B1). This plan promises to have a profound impact on the affordability of healthy food in the United States, as Wal-Mart is the largest grocer in the country. Its market position means that its capacity to change the foodscape rivals that of federal regulators. Wal-Mart has generally been considered the premier shopping venue for the underclass in America; blogs like People of Wal-Mart (peopleofwalmart.com) fixate on the store's lowbrow clientele, offering visual evidence of their alleged tackiness. Outside of those subcultural spaces that value rock-bottom prices at the cost of ethical business practices, there is not a great deal of cultural capital forthcoming for Wal-Mart shoppers.

However, the Obama-backed initiative brings elements of privileged foodways—namely, healthy foods—into the reach of the American underclass, in the same way Wal-Mart has made available the consumer-goods signifiers of luxury (large flat-screen televisions, for example) that used to connote privilege. In doing so, it represents a hybrid space marked by an infusion of the "high" into the "low." Although critics may fairly charge that Wal-Mart's way of doing business depresses wages, it is hard to argue that their infusion of elements of privileged foodways will not dramatically reshape what privileged and resistant foodways even mean. It may become more difficult to claim culinary capital for eating healthy food, as such food becomes widely available and affordable.

If hybridity at Wal-Mart is about the infusion of the "high" into the "low," at Whole Foods it is the other way around. Whole Foods's tagline, "Selling the Highest Quality Natural and Organic Products," clarifies its mission and its potential as a source of culinary capital for its shoppers, who can earn distinction by accessing the privileged food discourses it consolidates. Buzzwords like "green," "sustainability," "community," and "whole planet" crowd the store's description of its values on its website. But, like just about any retailer that hopes to make a killing in the marketplace, Whole Foods is concerned with giving its customers what they want to eat, and so it sells many products that emerge from lowbrow or resistant foodscapes. Whither the organic Twinkie? The sustainably produced chicken nugget? The healthy white bread? Aisles four, ten, and one, respectively. Whole Foods puts a wholesome, healthy spin on such "junk" foods, no doubt, but its inclusive embrace of them at all throws into question their presumed unsuitability for garnering culinary capital. Whole Foods as hybrid foodscape stands to move "junk" from its marginalized status, thereby changing the criteria by which one seeks culinary capital.

Hybrid Food Programming

Finally, we have also identified a hybridization of high and low food practices in the most recent trends in food-related television programming. As we discussed in chapter 3, media are quick to adapt in ways that respond to shifting desires and demands from their audience. This is evident, for example, in Food Network programming that has become increasingly focused on saving money in addition to—or even in place of—saving time. From shows like *Sandra's Money Saving Meals* and *Ten Dollar Dinners with Melissa d'Arabian* to articles featured on the network's website, including "Holiday Values: High Flavor, Low Cost," "5 Cost-Saving Tips to Entertain in Style this Holiday Season," "Melissa's Top 8 Money-Saving Tips for Thanksgiving," "Melissa's Top 7 Money-Saving Tricks for the Holidays," "Sandra's Money Saving Tips," and "Ask Aida: Saving Money," the network's programming and website reflects an awareness of shifting priorities among an audience that may be more focused on economic insecurity than on conforming to privileged food practices. At the same time, this focus on cost goes hand-in-hand with a continuing commitment to healthy eating. Just as the Food Network programming we discussed in chapter 3 sought to provide help to the over-stressed mother who wanted to provide her family with healthy meals despite growing demands on her time, these recent trends offer similar solutions to consumers who seek to balance their desire for healthy eating with the reality of limited budgets. In doing so, they merge a focus on health that usually comes with a significant price tag with a cost consciousness that would typically lead consumers to rely on unhealthy fast food or industrially produced food.

At the same time, we identify a second trend in food-related television that also reflects hybridization of high and low eating practices, namely an increased focus on and celebration of pleasure and overindulgence. We speculate that at a time of financial uncertainty, television producers and advertisers surmise that their audience may be more likely to seek escape and to indulge in fantasy through food. Such programming has become a hallmark of the Travel Channel, which has enjoyed success with shows like *No Reservations with Anthony Bourdain* as it indulges viewers' desires for exotic escape through food, and *Man v. Food*, in which host Adam Richman travels across the country attempting various food challenges that require him to eat excessive amounts of food or excessively hot and spicy dishes. For an audience that may be tired of hearing about the need to make healthy food choices and to control one's diet, Richman's show offers relief. One recent iteration of the show, *Man v. Food: Carnivore Chronicles*, follows Richman as he seeks out the "meatiest meals" that the country has to offer. For an audience that has been inundated with advice from those "in the know" to eat less meat, a show like Richman's can serve as an escape from such mandates while its popularity may also signal a rejection of those very "food rules." Like *Man v. Food*, the Travel Channel's *Paradise* series also celebrates indulgence, excess, and pleasure in one's food choices. With episodes that celebrate breakfast paradise, diner paradise, sandwich paradise, deep-fried paradise, buffet paradise, steak paradise, and all-you-can-eat paradise, this series can hardly be read as promoting a set of privileged eating practices that emphasize health and dietary restraint. Instead, this show invites its audience to reject such mandates in favor of excess and overindulgence. While such programming could be read as offering its viewers a necessary escape from calls for more restrained eating practices, we speculate that the growing presence and popularity of such shows points to a more sustained hybridization of privileged and resistant food practices.

DISSENT, DEMOCRACY, AND CONSUMER CITIZENSHIP

If, as we have argued, the promise of culinary capital can shape individual and group identities, then it can function to both reinforce and challenge prevailing values and ideologies. In fact, what may begin as "resistance" to privileged food practices may eventually impact the culinary landscape in more sustained ways. Unlike the space of the fair, what we see in these hybrid foodways is not merely a temporary escape from one realm—in that case, privileged food-topia—to another realm, junk-land. Rather, these hybrid foodways show the "high" and the "low" transforming themselves from within as they respond to the demands of consumer citizens who seek to balance pleasure with responsibility, excess with restraint, and to be rewarded for their efforts with food they like and with status for having made the effort. Such reshaping of the marketplace of the "high" and the "low" makes different choices available on a regular basis, thus removing the economic obstacles and sense of absurdity for those who might want to participate in privileged foodways, and eliminating the shame for those who might want to resist them. The result is that that what counts as the privileged and the resistant foodways transform, a change wrought by consumer citizens who remake themselves as they remake their food desires and practices.

While we have identified two distinct paths to culinary capital, one that requires adherence to a set of privileged food practices and one that promotes food practices that run counter to them, we conclude that the continual interplay between these two seemingly conflicting options invites would-be consumer citizens to play an active role in shaping and reshaping the capitalist marketplace. Such a model of consumer citizenship offers a productive means for dealing with the machinery of capitalism and industrial foodways when opting out entirely is impractical or undesirable. In particular, we want to think about the potential impact on the contemporary foodscape of such consumer citizenship and, more specifically, to consider its potential for reshaping the privileged food practices through which culinary capital is earned. We do so by situating this discussion within the broader framework of the role of dissent within a legitimate democracy.

Dissent has long been understood as a central feature of democratic citizenship and responsible politics. Rather than destabilizing strong democracies, it helps them to navigate a path between "submissive quiescence" and "violent resistance" (Ivie 2005, 279), either of which would signal dysfunction. Dissent can be most powerfully be enacted "by converting everyday practices such as reading and talking into clever tactical maneuvers" (Ivie 2005, 281), thus "turning the tables on the powerful" (De Certeau quoted in Ivie 2005, 281). Extending this list of everyday practices to include one's food practices, we argue that individual choices that run counter to current food orthodoxy can be read initially as productive acts of dissent against a seemingly monolithic culinary landscape. Rather than castigating consumers who engage in food practices that defy the established ethos, we argue that they exercise a kind of consumer citizenship that promotes an alternative path to culinary capital that has the potential to reshape the culinary landscape.

Before we plan for the culinary revolution, however, we must take into account the nature of dissent within the context of a healthy and legitimate democracy. Ivie warns us against adopting a "heroic model of dissent that postulates some Atlas-like figure overturning a world, or even a regime, of injustice," suggesting instead that we consider "how existing power relations might be rendered problematic and transformed over time in a boundary-crossing process of disruptive speaking and writing" (2005, 282). To this list of potentially disruptive acts we would add "eating" as we argue that crossing the boundary between privileged and non-privileged food practices should be read as a small-scale form of dissent that may over time yield greater results than larger-scale efforts.

The challenge posed by the 1960s countercuisine that we discussed in chapter 1, for example, was contained as its practices, if not its egalitarian ideals, were absorbed into the capitalist marketplace, ironically providing the very terminology that would shape the highly lucrative contemporary foodscape. As we have seen, capitalist re-appropriation is also at work in state fairs, competitive eating contests, and "junk" food blogs, where vendors and corporate sponsors profit from marketing excess to a consuming public desperate to evade prevailing mandates for "healthy" and "restrained" eating.

At the same time, given the flexibility and adaptability of culinary capital, we conclude that it offers a path for moving beyond a form of dissent that serves merely to reinforce those privileged practices that dominate the current culinary and cultural landscape. Rather, culinary capital should be recognized as a crucial means of empowering citizen consumers who pursue alternative paths to it, manifested particularly in the sites of hybridization we have examined. In other words, what may initially appear as dissent against contemporary food orthodoxy must be recognized as having the potential to effect change in those food practices that are privileged at least in part because they promise culinary capital to those who adhere to them. As consumer citizens across the economic and cultural spectrum make food choices that integrate privileged and unprivileged practices alike, they potentially transform the culinary landscape and utilize the power of culinary capital to do so.

Notes

Chapter 2

1. At one meal assembly business at which the authors conducted research, the preparation and cleanup were done exclusively by the franchise owners, who were an upper middle-class white couple. This franchise went out of business in 2010.
2. e-Grocers are linked to this history to the extent that they increasingly market prepared meals that require little more than heating up before being served. We discuss this trend in more detail in this chapter.
3. This begs questions about the fate of present-day meal assembly businesses in the midst of our severe economic recession.
4. See Hartmann (1981) for more on the idea that women's wages, when spent on substitute products or labor, do not actually translate into reduced work weeks on the domestic front.
5. An important exception to this is "homemaker entrepreneurs/momtrepreneurs"—artisanal brownie bakers, cottage cheese industrialists, and the like who toil in a domestic setting but get pay and publicity for their efforts.
6. It is interesting to consider contemporary meal assembly kitchens in contrast with the "British Restaurants" of the 1940s and 1950s in the United Kingdom described by Marion Roberts—cafeterias that sought to provide working-class people with balanced, nutritious, and convenient meals. They were state-run, which stirred up anxieties about women being unable to fulfill their proper role in cooking for men (Roberts 1984, 114). "The need for the restaurants was argued in terms of reducing the burden of housewives' work at home, rather than (as had been proposed at the restaurants' inception) to resolve the contradictions between women's responsibilities for domestic work in the home and the expansion of the female labour force" (115). Roberts notes that communal work stands to erode the most pleasurable aspect of the work of housewives—its relative autonomy (118).
7. Typical twelve-"meal" assembly packages range from about $225 to $250; each "meal" serves four to six people. But the "meals" are only entrees, and sides cost extra, thus driving up the cost of a full meal well beyond the range of most fast and processed food, and certainly beyond the price of meals that result from planning, shopping, and cooking at home.

Chapter 3

1. Of course, viewers are capable of counter-hegemonic readings of any of these Food Network texts. While our intention in this chapter is to analyze the texts themselves, rather than their reception, our focus on resistant food practices in later chapters acknowledges divergent possibilities.

2. This is not to suggest that viewers of *Paula's Home Cooking* or *Giada at Home* are members of the leisure class. In fact, it is likely the ability to imagine having the time to do what Deen and De Laurentiis do that draws in working- and middle-class fans who seek a thirty-minute flight of fantasy from their busy lives. See Bower (2004) for more on the phenomenon of food texts as fodder for escape, rather than instruction.

3. Such debates are not exclusive to the realm of food television. Laura Shapiro notes their genesis in a war of words between food writers and cookbook authors (rather than TV chefs) in the 1930s and 1940s, epitomized by traditionalist James Beard and food-industry-friendly Poppy Cannon. "Beard believed the housewife was losing her way, forfeiting her skills, mindlessly surrendering to packaged foods whenever they beckoned. Cannon saw that same housewife heading smartly into the future, reinventing great culinary traditions with the help of epicurean new products" (Shapiro 2004, 5).

Chapter 4

1. This is true not only of sites that are dedicated exclusively to restaurant reviews but also to those sites that include such reviews within the broader framework of "lifestyle guides." Both Citysearch and Yelp, for example, emphasize member participation as central to their success. Citysearch identifies its mission as "help[ing] people make informed decisions about where to spend their time and money by delivering trusted content, local expertise, and useful tools—including 14.5 million business listings, over 600,000 user reviews, and ratings on over 2 million business locations nationwide." Yelp defines itself as "an online urban city guide that helps people find cool places to eat, shop, drink, relax and play, based on the informed opinions of a vibrant and active community of locals in the know."

2. It is noteworthy that chowhounds set themselves up against users of the *Zagat Guide*, rather than against users of more typical "expert" criticism like that of newspaper critics. *Zagat* bills itself as democratic and inclusive due to its practice of amalgamating comments from readers/eaters, rather than relying on paid authorities. Priscilla Parkhurst Ferguson calls the *Zagat Guide* a "plebiscite" model of food criticism, which means that it is based on the combined opinions of regular diners (as opposed to "judges" like

Craig Claiborne and Ruth Reichl or "tribunals" like the Michelin Guide). "Founded in 1979 by Tim and Nina Zagat and some two hundred of their friends, the Zagat survey was the first, and remains the foremost, publication to issue an open call for diners' opinions, regardless of their training, knowledge, or background. Zagat, its advocates claim, is democracy in action" (Ferguson 2008, 52).

Chapter 5

1. The authors conducted 45 interviews, many in family/friend small group clusters, at the 2009 Indiana State Fair, eliciting the perspectives of 117 fairgoers. Interviews were conducted in a bench-laden promenade on the fairgrounds lined by food stands, where the casual seating arrangements and relaxed atmosphere made interviewees receptive to our questions. Almost all interviewees were eating, or had just finished eating, as we spoke with them. The interviewees were roughly evenly split along gender lines, and ranged in age from six to mid-seventies; they hailed primarily from within the state of Indiana, though approximately 5 percent of interviewees were visiting the fair from out of state.
2. The authors reviewed vendor and concession application templates from ten states (Alabama, California, Indiana, Kansas, Kentucky, Minnesota, Missouri, New Mexico, New York, and Wyoming) in 2010.
3. In our sample of ten state fairs, Indiana was not alone in its ambivalent privileging of health and excess. The Kentucky State Fair also emphasizes its "Healthy Horizons" program, "a celebration of healthy people living healthy lives!" (Kentucky State Fair website) that offers on-site screenings and a blood drive. Other states in our sample (New York, Minnesota) had what we would describe as more low-key health and medical exhibits, without articulating them under the larger rubric of a state-sanctioned health or wellness initiative.
4. We conducted twelve interviews of couples or family/friend/colleague clusters at the contest, yielding the perspective of thirty different people. Twenty-five of the interviewees were spectators, and five were ESPN employees working at the event.
5. We interviewed six competitive eaters and six fans at the event.
6. We note the attempt at humor here, as humans did not inhabit the Earth during the Mesozoic era in which dinosaurs existed.
7. For more on this link between religion and food, see Rozin (1987) and Sack (2000).

Works Cited

Abrahams, Roger, and Richard Bauman. 1977. "Toward an Enactment-Centered Theory of Folklore." In *Frontiers in Folklore*, edited by William R. Bascom, 79–120. Boulder, CO: Westview Press.

Adema, Pauline. 2009. *Garlic Capital of the World: Gilroy, Garlic, and the Making of a Festive Foodscape.* Jackson: University of Mississippi Press.

Adler, Thomas A. 1988. "Bluegrass Music and Meal-Fried Potatoes: Food, Festival, Community." In *We Gather Together: Food and Festival in American Life*, edited by Theodore C. Humphrey and Lin T. Humphrey, 195–204. Ann Arbor: UMI Research Press.

Ashley, Bob, Joanne Hollows, Steve Jones, and Ben Taylor. 2004. *Food and Cultural Studies.* London: Routledge.

Bakhtin, Mikhail. 1984. *Rabelais and His World.* Translated by Hélène Iswolsky. Bloomington: Indiana University Press.

Beezley, William H., Cheryl English Martin, and William E. French. 1994. "Introduction: Constructing Consent, Inciting Conflict." In *Rituals of Rule, Rituals of Resistance: Public Celebrations of Popular Culture in Mexico*, edited by William H. Beezley, Cheryl English Martin, and William E. French, xiii–xxxii. Wilmington, DE: SR Books.

Belasco, Warren. 1989. *Appetite for Change: How the Counterculture Took On the Food Industry, 1966–1988.* New York: Pantheon.

Belasco, Warren. 2005. "Food and the Counterculture: A Story of Bread and Politics." In *The Cultural Politics of Food and Eating: A Reader*, edited by James Watson and Melissa Caldwell, 217–234. Malden, MA: Blackwell.

Bell, David. 2002. "Fragments for a New Urban Culinary Geography." *Journal for the Study of Food and Society* 6(1):10–21.

Bourdieu, Pierre. 1984. *Distinction: A Social Critique of the Judgement of Taste.* Translated by Richard Nice. Cambridge, MA: Harvard University Press.

Bourdieu, Pierre. 1985. "The Social Space and the Genesis of Groups." *Theory and Society* 14(6):723–744.

Bourdieu, Pierre, and Loïc Wacquant. 1992. *An Invitation to Reflexive Sociology.* Chicago: University of Chicago Press.

Bower, Anne L. 2004. "Romanced by Cookbooks." *Gastronomica* 4(2):35–42.

Bugge, Annechen Bahr, and Reidar Almas. 2006. "Domestic Dinner: Representations and Practices of a Proper Meal among Young Suburban Mothers." *Journal of Consumer Culture* 6(2):203–228.

Calhoun, Craig, and Richard Sennett. 2007. *Practicing Cultures.* New York: Routledge.

Carnall, Ryan. 2009. Interview by authors. Mount Laurel, New Jersey, August 1.

Carrington, Christopher. 2008. "Feeding Lesbigay Families." In *Food and Culture: A Reader, Second Edition*, edited by Carole Counihan and Penny Van Esterik, 259–286. New York: Routledge.

Cole, C. L. 2008. "Bounding American Empire: Sport, Sex, and Politics." In *Youth Culture and Sport: Identity, Power, and Politics*, edited by Michael D. Giardina and Michele K. Donnelly, 55–68. New York: Routledge.

Collins, Glenn. 2008. "A Critic, Insatiable and Dismissed." *New York Times*, November 25:D1.

Collins, Kathleen. 2008. "TV Cooking Shows: The Evolution of a Genre." FlowTV 7.13, Special Features, May 7. Accessed January 12, 2009. http://flowtv.org/?p=1316.

Collins, Kathleen. 2009. *Watching What We Eat: The Evolution of Television Cooking Shows.* New York: Continuum.

Collins, Micah. 2009. Interview by authors. Island Park, New York, May 25.

Conti, Crazy Legs. 2009. Interview by authors. Island Park, New York, May 25.

Coontz, Stephanie. 1992. *The Way We Never Were: American Families and the Nostalgia Trap.* New York: Basic Books.

Corfe, Robert. 2007. *Populism Against Progress and the Collapse of Aspirational Values.* Bury St. Edmunds, UK: Arena.

Coveney, John. 2000. *Food, Morals and Meaning: The Pleasure and Anxiety of Eating.* London: Routledge.

Cowan, Ruth Schwartz. 1983. *More Work for Mother: The Ironies of Household Technology from the Open Hearth to the Microwave.* New York: Basic.

Daniels, Arlene Kaplan. 1987. "Invisible Work." *Social Problems* 34(5):403–415.

DeVault, Marjorie L. 1991. *Feeding the Family: The Social Organization of Caring as Gendered Work.* Chicago: University of Chicago Press.

Douglas, Mary. 1999. "Deciphering a Meal [1972]." In *Implicit Meanings.* London: Routledge.

Epstein, Joseph. 2002. *Snobbery: The American Version.* Boston: Houghton Mifflin.

Fagone, Jason. 2006. *Horsemen of the Esophagus: Competitive Eating and the Big Fat American Dream.* New York: Three Rivers Press.

Falassi, Alessandro. 1987. "Festival: Definition and Morphology." In *Time Out of Time: Essays on the Festival*, edited by Alessandro Falassi, 1–10. Albuquerque: University of New Mexico Press.

Featherstone, Mike. 1991. *Consumer Culture and Postmodernism.* London: Sage.

Ferguson, Priscilla Parkhurst. 2008. "Michelin in America." *Gastronomica* 8(1):49–55.

Floyd, Janet. 2004. "Coming Out of the Kitchen: Texts, Contexts and Debates." *cultural geographies* 10:61–73.

Foucault, Michel. 1980. *Power/Knowledge: Selected Interviews & Other Writing 1972–1977*. Edited by Colin Gordon. New York: Pantheon Books.

Foucault, Michel. 1990. *The History of Sexuality: An Introduction,* vol. 1. Translated by Robert Hurley. New York: Vintage.

Friedan, Betty. 1963. *The Feminine Mystique.* New York: Dell.

Frumkin, Paul. 2007. "Everyone's a Critic: Operators Adapt to Surge in Online Reviews by Patrons." *Nation's Restaurant News*, January 8:1, 39–40, 42.

Gans, Herbert J. 2007. "Everyday News, Newsworkers, and Professional Journalism." *Political Communication* 24(2):161–166.

Gerbner, George, and Larry Gross. 1976. "Living With Television: The Violence Profile." *Journal of Communication* 26(2):172–199.

Gilman, Charlotte Perkins. 1898/1966. *Women and Economics.* New York: Harper Torchbook.

Glassner, Barry. 2007. *The Gospel of Food: Everything You Think You Know about Food Is Wrong.* New York: Harper Collins.

Goodyear, Dana. 2010. "Killer Food: Hollywood Lines Up For Bacon, Head Cheese, and Spam." *New Yorker* (April 26):34–37.

Greene, Carlnita P. 2011. "Competing Identities at the Table: Slow Food, Consumption, and the Performance of Social Style." In *Food as Communication/Communication as Food*, edited by Janet M. Cramer, Lynn M. Walter, and Carlnita P. Greene, 75–94. New York: Peter Lang.

Gussow, Joan Dye. 1987. "The Fragmentation of Need: Women, Food and Marketing." *Heresies* 21:39–43.

Halberstam, Judith. 1998. *Female Masculinity.* Durham, NC: Duke University Press.

Halloran, Vivian Nun. 2004. "Biting Reality: Extreme Eating and the Fascination with the Gustatory Abject." *Iowa Journal of Cultural Studies* 4:27–42. Accessed March 30, 2010. http://www.iowa.edu/~ijcs/mainstream/halloran.htm.

Halter, Marilyn. 2000. *Shopping for Identity: The Marketing of Ethnicity.* New York: Schocken Books.

Hansen, Signe. 2008. "Society of the Appetite." *Food, Culture & Society* 11(1):49–67.

Hartmann, Heidi I. 1981. "The Family as the Locus of Gender, Class, and Political Struggle: The Example of Housework." *Signs* 6(3):366–394.

Harvest of Fear: Exploring the Growing Fight Over Genetically Modified Food. 2001. A Frontline/Nova Special Presentation. Written, produced, and directed by Jon Palfreman. Original airdate: April 23, 2001. Accessed November 21, 2009. Transcript available at http://www.pbs.org/wgbh/harvest/etc/script.html.

Hayden, Dolores. 1981. *The Grand Domestic Revolution: A History of Feminist Designs for American Homes, Neighborhoods, and Cities.* Cambridge, MA: MIT Press.

Heldke, Lisa M. 2003. *Exotic Appetites: Ruminations of a Food Adventurer.* New York: Routledge.

Hochschild, Arlie Russell. 1989/2003. *The Second Shift.* New York: Penguin.

Holden, T.J.M. 2005. "The Overcooked and Underdone: Masculinities in Japanese Food Programming." *Food and Foodways: Men, Food and Asian Identities* 13(1–2):39–65.

Holliday, Laura Scott. 2001. "Kitchen Technologies: Promises and Alibis, 1944–1966." *Camera Obscura* 16(2):79–131.

hooks, bell. 1992. *Black Looks: Race and Representation.* Boston: South End Press.

Huber, Bettina. 1999. "Experts in Organizations: The Power of Expertise." Paper presented at the Academy of Business and Administrative Science Conference, Barcelona, July. Accessed June 20, 2010. http://www.sba.muohio.edu/abas/1999/huberbe.pdf.

Hutcheon, Linda. 1995. *Irony's Edge: The Theory and Politics of Irony.* New York: Routledge.

Hyman, Gwen. 2008. "The Taste of Fame: Chefs, Diners, Celebrity, Class." *Gastronomica* 8(3):43–52.

Inness, Sherrie. 2001. *Dinner Roles: American Women and Culinary Culture.* Iowa City: University of Iowa Press.

Ivie, Robert L. 2005. "Democratic Dissent and the Trick of Rhetorical Critique." *Cultural Studies—Critical Methodologies* 5:276–293.

Jarvis, Ed "Cookie". 2009. Interview by authors. Island Park, New York, May 25.

Jayaraman, Saru. 2011. "Restaurants and Race: Discrimination and Disparity in the Food Service Sector." *Race, Poverty and the Environment: A Journal for Social and Environmental Justice* 18(1). Accessed January 23, 2012. http://urbanhabitat.org/18–1/jayaraman.

Johnson, Adrienne Rose. 2012. "The Magic Metabolisms of Competitive Eating." In *Taking Food Public: Redefining Foodways in a Changing World*, edited by Psyche Williams-Forson and Carole Counihan, 279–292. New York: Routledge.

Johnston, Josée, and Shyon Baumann. 2010. *Foodies: Democracy and Distinction in the Gourmet Foodscape.* New York: Routledge.

Julier, Alice, and Laura Lindenfeld. 2005. "Mapping Men onto the Menu: Masculinities and Food." *Food and Foodways* 13(1):1–16.

Keeler, Russ. 2009. Interview by authors. Island Park, New York, May 25.

Keller, James R., and Leslie Stratyner, eds. 2005. *New Queer Aesthetics on Television: Essays on Recent Programming.* Jefferson, NC: McFarland & Company.

Kemmer, Debbie. 2000. "Tradition and Change in Domestic Roles and Food Preparation." *Sociology* 34(2):323–333.

Kessler, David. 2009. *The End of Overeating: Taking Control of the Insatiable American Appetite.* Emmaus, PA: Rodale.

Ketchum, Cheri. 2005. "The Essence of Cooking Shows: How the Food Network Constructs Consumer Fantasies." *Journal of Communication Inquiry* 29(3):217–234.

Ketchum, Cheri. 2007. "Tunnel Vision and Food: A Political-Economic Analysis of Food Network." In *Cable Visions: Television Beyond Broadcasting*, edited by Sarah Banet-Weiser, Cynthia Chris, and Anthony Freitas, 158–176. New York: New York University Press.

Kirkland, Anna. 2011. "The Environmental Account of Obesity: A Case for Feminist Skepticism." *Signs: Journal of Women in Culture and Society,* 36(2):411–436.

Kirshenblatt-Gimblett, Barbara. 1999. "Playing to the Senses: Food as a Performance Medium." *Performance Research* 4(1):1–30.

Kuhn, Mary Ellen. 2009. "Building a New Model for Meal Assembly." *Food Technology Magazine*, online exclusives, February. Accessed May 10, 2010. http://members.ift.org/IFT/Pubs/FoodTechnology/OnlineExclusive/mealassembly.htm.

Laurence, Charles. 2002. "Eating is US 'Sport of the Future'." *Telegraph* (UK), September 15. Accessed February 21, 2010. http://www.telegraph.co.uk/news/worldnews/northamerica/usa/1407287/Eating-is-US-sport-of-the-future.html.

LeBesco, Kathleen. 2004. *Revolting Bodies?: The Struggle to Redefine Fat Identity.* Amherst: University of Massachusetts Press.

LeBesco, Kathleen, and Peter Naccarato. 2008. "Julia Child, Martha Stewart and the Rise of Culinary Capital." In *Edible Ideologies: Representing Food and Meaning*, edited by Kathleen LeBesco and Peter Naccarato, 223–238. Albany: State University of New York Press.

Levmore, Saul, and Martha C. Nussbaum. 2011. *The Offensive Internet: Speech, Privacy, and Reputation.* Cambridge, MA: Harvard University Press.

Lindenfeld, Laura. 2010. "On the Ethics of Food Television: Does Rachael Ray Really Promote Healthy Eating?" In *Whose Weight Is It Anyway: Essays On Ethics and Eating*, edited by I. de Beaufort, Sofie Vandamme, and Suzanne van de Vathorst, 161–173. Gent: Acco Peer Reviewed Series.

Mannur, Anita. 2007. "Culinary Nostalgia: Authenticity, Nationalism, and Diaspora." *MELUS* 32(4):11–31.

Marwick, Alice. 2007. "The People's Republic of YouTube?: Interrogating Rhetorics of Internet Democracy." Paper presented at Association of Internet Researchers Annual Conference, Vancouver, CA.

McConnon, Aili. 2008. "Salad Days for Web Grocers." *BusinessWeek*, September 15:16.

McCullen, Christie. 2011. "The White Farm Imaginary: How One Farmers Market *Refetishizes* the Production of Food and Limits Food Politics." In *Food as Communication/ Communication as Food*, edited by Janet M. Cramer, Lynn M. Walter, and Carlnita P. Greene, 217–234. New York: Peter Lang.

Miller, Toby. 2007. *Cultural Citizenship: Cosmopolitanism, Consumerism, and Television in a Neoliberal Age*. Philadelphia: Temple University Press.

Moran, Joe. 2005. "Hum, Ping, Rip: The Sounds of Cooking." *New Statesman*, January 24.

Mullen, Megan. 2008. " 'Everybody Eats': The Food Network and Symbolic Capital." In *Food for Thought: Essays on Eating and Culture*, edited by Lawrence C. Rubin, 113–124. Jefferson, NC: McFarland.

Murcott, Anne. 1997. "Family Meals—A Thing of the Past?" In *Food, Health and Identity*, edited by Pat Caplan, 32–49. London: Routledge.

Nader, Ralph. 2003. "Signs of a Societal Decay." *Nader.org*, October 24. Accessed February 21, 2010. http://www.nader.org/index.php?/archives/166-Signs-of-a-Societal-Decay.html.

Nerz, Ryan. 2006. *Eat This Book: A Year of Gorging and Glory on the Competitive Eating Circuit*. New York: St. Martin's Press.

Neuhaus, Jessamyn. 1999. "The Way to a Man's Heart: Gender Roles, Domestic Ideology, and Cookbooks in the 1950s." *Journal of Social History* 32(3):529–555.

Neuhaus, Jessamyn. 2003. *Manly Meals and Mom's Home Cooking: Cookbooks and Gender in Modern America*. Baltimore: Johns Hopkins University Press.

Nutter, Kathleen Banks. 2008. "From Romance to PMS: Images of Women and Chocolate in Twentieth-Century America." In *Edible Ideologies: Representing Food and Meaning*, edited by Kathleen LeBesco and Peter Naccarato, 199–221. Albany: State University of New York Press.

O'Connor, John. 2007. "Feeding Frenzy—The Rise of Competitive Eating." *Culinate.com,* January 15. Accessed February 21, 2010. http://www.culinate.com/articles/features/Feeding+frenzy.

Opie, Frederick Douglass. 2008. *Hog and Hominy: Soul Food From Africa to America*. New York: Columbia University Press.

Ouellette, Laurie, and James Hay. 2008. *Better Living through Reality TV: Television and Post-Welfare Citizenship*. Hoboken, NJ: Wiley-Blackwell.

Parasecoli, Fabio. 2008. *Bite Me: Food in Popular Culture*. New York: Berg.

Patel, Raj, Eric Holt-Gimenez, and Annie Shattuck. 2009. "Ending Africa's Hunger." *Nation*, September 21. Accessed October 20, 2009. http://www.thenation.com/doc/20090921/patel_et_al.

Pattillo, Mary. 2010. *Black on the Block: The Politics of Race and Class in the City*. Chicago: University of Chicago Press.

Peed, Michael. 2009. "Bark Hot Dogs." *New Yorker*, December 14. Accessed June 27, 2010. http://www.newyorker.com/arts/reviews/tables/2009/12/14/091214gota_GOAT_tables_peed.

Peterson, Richard A. 1997. "The Rise and Fall of Highbrow Snobbery as a Status Marker." *Poetics* 25:75–92.

Pogue, David. 2008. "Grocery Shopping Made Easy." *New York Times*, June 19:1.

Pollan, Michael. 2006. *The Omnivore's Dilemma*. New York: Penguin.

Pollan, Michael. 2009. *Food Rules: An Eater's Manual*. New York: Penguin.

Putnam, Robert. 2000. *Bowling Alone: The Collapse and Revival of American Community*. New York: Simon and Schuster.

Ray, Krishnendu. 2007. "Domesticating Cuisine: Food and Aesthetics on American Television." *Gastronomica* 7(1):50–63.

Redden, Guy. 2007. "Makeover Morality and Consumer Culture." In *Makeover Television: Realities Remodelled*, edited by Dana Heller, 150–164. London; New York: I.B. Tauris & Co.

Retzinger, Jean P. 2008. "The Embodied Rhetoric of 'Health' from Farm Fields to Salad Bowls." In *Edible Ideologies: Representing Food and Meaning*, edited by Kathleen LeBesco and Peter Naccarato, 149–178. Albany: State University of New York Press.

Richardson, Brenda. 2009. Interview by authors. Indianapolis, Indiana, August 8.

Roberts, Marion. 1984. "Private Kitchens, Public Cooking." In *Making Space: Women and the Man-Made Environment*, edited by Matrix, 106–119. London: Pluto.

Rose, Nikolas. 1999. *Powers of Freedom: Reframing Political Thought*. Cambridge: Cambridge University Press.

Rose, Toby, and Harriet Arkell. 2003. "Top French Chef Kills Himself." *London Evening Standard*, February 25. Accessed June 19, 2009. http://www.thisislondon.co.uk/news/article3554625details/Top+French+chef+kills+himself+/article.do.

Rousseau, Signe. 2012. *Food Media: Celebrity Chefs and the Politics of Everyday Interference*. New York: Berg.

Rozin, Paul. 1987. "Sweetness, Sensuality, Sin, Safety and Socialization: Some Speculations." In *Sweetness*, edited by J. Dobbing, 99–110. London: Springer Verlag.

Rozin, Paul. 1997. "Moralization." In *Morality and Health*, edited by Allan M. Brandt and Paul Rozin, 379–401. New York: Routledge.

Rubin, Lawrence C. 2008. "Beyond Bread and Circuses: Professional Competitive Eating." In *Food For Thought: Essays on Eating and Culture*, edited by Lawrence Rubin, 248–263. Jefferson, NC: McFarland & Co.

Sack, Daniel. 2000. *Whitebread Protestants: Food and Religion in American Culture*. New York: Palgrave.

Sayer, Liana C. 2005. "Gender, Time and Inequality: Trends in Women's and Men's Paid Work, Unpaid Work and Free Time." *Social Forces* 84(1):285–303.

Shapiro, Laura. 2004. *Something From the Oven: Reinventing Dinner in 1950s America*. New York: Viking.

Sietsema, Robert. 2010. "Everyone Eats . . . But That Doesn't Make You a Restaurant Critic." *Columbia Journalism Review*, January/February. Accessed March 9, 2010. http://www.cjr.org/feature/everyone_eats.php?page=all.

Skidelsky, William. 2005. "So, What's the Food Like?" *New Statesman*, September 5: 14–15.

Solomon, Deborah. 2009. "Questions for Ruth Reichl: Clearing the Table." *New York Times Magazine*, October 18:18.

Sorensen, Tom. 2009. "Here's Appreciating Competitive Eating, and Tasty Food Again." *TradingMarkets.com*, July 3. Accessed February 21, 2010. http://www.tradingmarkets.com/.site/news/Stock%20News/2404603/.

Spigel, Lynn. 1992. *Make Room for TV: Television and the Family Ideal in Postwar America*. Chicago: University of Chicago Press.

Spitznagel, Eric. 1999. *The Junk Food Companion: The Complete Guide to Eating Badly*. New York: Plume.

Stallybrass, Peter, and Allon White. 1986. *The Politics & Poetics of Transgression*. New York: Cornell University Press.

Stark, J. 2007. "Appeal of Online Grocery Shopping." *Joplin Independent*, April 27. Accessed August 27, 2009. http://www.joplinindependent.com/display_article.php/jslack1177875355.

Stein, Joel. 2008. "Extreme Eating." *Time*, January 21:68.

Steingarten, Jeffrey. 1996. "The Omnivore: Learning to Eat Everything." *Slate.com*, August 28. Accessed May 10, 2010. http://www.slate.com/id/3152.

Stolberg, Sheryl Gay. 2011. "Wal-Mart Shifts Strategy to Promote Healthy Foods." *New York Times*, January 20:B1.

Swenson, Rebecca. 2007. "Kitchen Convergence: Televised Translations of Masculinity, Femininity and Food." Paper presented at National Communication Association Annual Convention, Chicago, November.

Swenson, Rebecca. 2009. "Domestic Divo? Televised Treatments of Masculinity, Femininity and Food." *Critical Studies in Media Communication* 26(1):36–53.

Tannahill, Reay. 1973. *Food in History*. New York: Stein and Day.

Thompson, John R. 2011. "Dinner Time Discourse: Convenience Foods and Industrial Society." In *Food as Communication/Communication as Food*, edited by Janet M. Cramer, Lynn M. Walter, and Carlnita P. Greene, 179–194. New York: Peter Lang.

Tumber, Howard. 2001. "Democracy in the Information Age: The Role of the Fourth Estate in Cyberspace." *Information, Communication & Society* 4(1):95–112.

U.S. Energy Information Administration. 2010. "Cooking Trends in the United States: Are We Really Becoming a Fast Food Country?" May 10. http://www.eia.doe.gov/emeu/recs/cookingtrends/cooking.html.

Veblen, Thorstein. 1899. *Theory of the Leisure Class: An Economic Study in the Evolution of Institutions.* New York: Macmillan.

Wagenvoord, Helen C. 2004. "The High Price of Cheap Food: Mealpolitik Over Lunch With Michael Pollan." *San Francisco Chronicle*, May 2. Accessed May 10, 2010. http://www.michaelpollan.com/press.php?id=8.

Warde, Alan. 1997. *Consumption, Food and Taste.* Thousand Oaks, CA: Sage.

Warde, Alan, Lydia Martens, and Wendy Olsen. 1999. "Consumption and the Problem of Variety: Cultural Omnivorousness, Social Distinction and Dining Out." *Sociology* 33(1):105–127.

Weinstein, Miriam. 2005. *The Surprising Power of Family Meals: How Eating Together Makes Us Smarter, Stronger, Healthier, and Happier.* Hanover, NH: Steerforth.

Whitmeyer, Joseph. 1996. "Eccentricity and Indulgence in Autocratic Rulers." *Sociological Perspectives* 39(1):59–83.

Williams-Forson, Psyche. 2012. "Other Women Cooked For My Husband: Negotiating Gender, Food, and Identities in an African American/Ghanaian Household." In *Taking Food Public: Redefining Foodways in a Changing World*, edited by Psyche Williams-Forson and Carole Counihan, 138–154. New York: Routledge.

Witherly, Steven A. 2007. *Why Humans Like Junk Food.* New York: iUniverse.

Witt, Doris. 2004. *Black Hunger: Soul Food and America.* Minneapolis: University of Minnesota Press.

Woods, Ronald B. 2007. *Social Issues in Sport.* Champaign, IL: Human Kinetics.

Woodward, Kath. 2009. *Embodied Sporting Practices: Regulating and Regulatory Bodies.* New York: Palgrave MacMillan.

Zukin, Sharon. 2008. "Consuming Authenticity: From Outposts of Difference to Means of Exclusion." *Cultural Studies* 22(5):724–748.

Index